APPIFY YOUR BUSINESS
by Bill Furlong

Digital | 978-1-944027-26-1
Soft | 978-1-944027-27-8

Net worlding
PUBLISHING

www.networlding.com

To my beautiful soul mate and wife, Peggy; our children Liam, Kylie, and Conor; and no less our pup, Piper. You inspire me every day.

# FOREWORD

After 35 years running companies, I've used a lot of business apps. In fact, I remember when these apps were called computer software. A past frustration in running my companies was not only the complexity of installing these applications, but the cost each time to buy them and integrate them into my business process. But there were ongoing problems, as none of these programs communicated directly with one another. As a result, it was always up to us to figure how to get the important data from one system to the other. And what made using these programs even more complex was that as my companies grew, we had to repeat the process all over again, regularly buying new software to keep up with our size.

This problem can largely be eliminated by today's business apps in the cloud. Companies can pay a small monthly fee to get started on a solution and then buy more as their businesses and customers grow. Today's apps can scale to almost every size business. In addition, there's an increased emphasis on data connectivity between apps. In this way, your company infrastructure is outsourced to a vendor in the cloud. This has several advantages, since that vendor now continues to develop the application with the latest advances in technology and functionality. They also provide the security around your company data that is required today.

Cloud apps have become a huge competitive advantage for small business owners, who can use the best software in the industry even when they're starting out. Plus, they can seamlessly scale their business both in terms of cost and functionality. These cloud apps can literally reinvent any company and put you on an even playing field with any larger business.

But choosing the right set of apps (or as it's referred to in this book, the *AppStack*) to create a seamless management system for your company must be done carefully. It's where many small business owners get stuck. This takes a carefully thought out strategy that this book, *Appify Your Company*, addresses. Bill Furlong shows you how to make effective strategic and tactical decisions when it comes to business apps. Equally as important, he guides you through the master dashboard that's needed to analyze the data so you can keep track of what's actually going on in your business. This puts you in the best position to make future decisions to leverage these results.

Want to grow your business profitably by leveraging technology? Read on.

Barry Moltz
Small Business Expert
www.barrymoltz.com

# REVIEWS

*"Bill Furlong has so thoroughly addressed one of the most underestimated aspects of running a business today: what apps to use, how, when, and why. As someone who runs a small business and works closely with entrepreneurs, this book hits home. It gives me clarity on how to be more productive and profitable, lays out a straightforward app strategy to execute, and addresses many critical questions I face daily. It's a reference manual that I'll keep coming back to and recommend to business founders and owners I know."*

- Raman Chadha, CEO Junto Institute

*"Appify Your Business is a refreshing take on how small business owners can act as their own IT system integrators with ease, rather than confusion. The clever handbook empowers us to amp up personal and business productivity by taming the jumbled mess of too much technology and not enough time. Bill Furlong also simplifies the language and shows us how to optimize apps in the cloud."*

- Marti Konstant, Founder, Konstant Change, training & consulting, investor, and best-selling author of Activate Your Agile Career

*"Bill's practical approach and guidance is what fast growing companies need to know about the power of apps. As one of the top mentors at Founder Institute Chicago, Bill continues to share his wisdom and entrepreneurial experience through this very hands-on book. Appify Your Business is a must read to get ahead."*

- Jason Jacobsohn, Managing Director, Founder Institute Chicago

*"This witty, urbane and delightful book flows like water as Bill Furlong guides the budding (or established) entrepreneur through the choppy acronym-laden sea of virtual tools that empower a business owner to take control and shape their company into a successful enterprise. Mr. Furlong explains, in common terms, how a fledgling entrepreneur can harness powerful apps, formerly affordable only by large corporations, to run his or her business. Whether you are at your desktop, or on a mobile device, this invaluable guide puts a powerful arsenal of digital tools at your disposal. Compelling and essential."*

- Greg Lochow, Owner Franklin Framing.  Retail, Printing, Design and Property Management Business Owner

*"Technology will be the competitive advantage for the small business owner.  Furlong simplifies what could be an intimating topic and makes creating your appstack approachable."*

- Kristi Zuhlke, CEO & Founder, KnowledgeHound

*"I am the CEO of a healthcare tech company and we use a myriad of software and vendor apps that can be overwhelming. This book provides an excellent technology overview for any company, discussing apps by category, plus a roadmap on how to best manage your tools and improve business. I especially like the simple action steps that are laid out by business objective. I recommend it to any business owner as a guide and an ongoing reference manual."*

- Evelyn Engert, CEO My Health and Money LLC

*"I am a veteran small business owner, not ready to retire, but no longer willing to put in the long hours in my various operations. Bill Furlong's Appify Your Business is a great primer for me, that guided me to keep my finger on the pulse of my operation. It seems that the App-centric work approach with the total view of my KPI metrics, is spot on. AYB provides the blueprint to organize my business apps, creating a global view of my financials, web analytics, social media, payroll, etc. If I have my smart phone in hand, I can use what I've learned in AYB to review my Executive Dashboard at home, on vacation, or even walking my dog. Great Read!"*

- Bob Hawkinson, CEO Hawkinson Nissan and Kia

*"In a world where the pace of business is moving at breakneck speed, business owners and managers are outmatched by time and technology. In his book Appify your Business, Bill Furlong moves to the frontline battle by showing owners and managers how to take back lost man-*

hours through "Appifying" your business. In exhaustive and yet poignant detail, Furlong takes you on an abridged version of what it's like to simply exist within the inefficiencies of dated technology processes and the struggling technologists who allow their companies to fall back while others advance. If you like to WIN and enjoy a good analytical, read then this book is for you. The author doesn't just highlight problems he brings solutions. If you want to quickly grow your business, create masterful efficiencies in your day parts, and launch your business to the next level then Appify Your Business is a must read. A winning formula from a winning business owner."

- Don Lindsay, Founder of Cauze

"I have been a small business tech entrepreneur for 17 years. We have seen it all and read it all over those years. Rarely does something catch your eye that truly synthesizes the disruptive technology of web-based applications. Appify Your Business' AppStack methodology is one I am convinced will be in every business owner's vernacular and incorporated into their business strategy and culture. This is an easy to understand "playbook" that helped me navigate my business through the web app review, selection and usage process and is making us more "disruptive" in the process."

- Dan Schramm, CEO Topiary

*"Lots of books for business men and women out there that are long on theory and short on practical advice. This is not one of those books. Appify makes the compelling case that by installing business apps within their critical departments, owners can manage and grow their businesses faster and more efficiently.*

*Bill Furlong has written a well-researched book that goes beyond just offering strategic reasons why business owners should rely on apps. He provides practical solutions by naming specific apps and showing how they can be of benefit. Appify is also full of solid management advice that new and experienced business owners alike will find extremely useful. Bill's tips on privacy and data collection, as well as marketing and social media are just two examples.*

*If you're looking for ways to grow your customer base and increase retention through better management of your business processes and systems – Appify is the book for you."*

- Lou Morales, President the Catnip Times


*"As a former colleague and new entrepreneur, I have found Bill's insights, guidance, and tools tremendously beneficial. The best part about the book is you don't have to read it from cover to cover. Just dive into the parts you need when you need it. Eventually, you'll read the whole thing. I am so glad he is sharing his experience through this book and SquareStack."*

- Allison Arden, Former Ad Age Publisher, Author of The Book of Doing, Entrepreneur

*Mr. Furlong's immense experience and passion shine through in his book "Appify Your Business." Time management and utilizing your companies' financial resources in the most productive form is crucial to a company's success. Appify Your Success provides a concise and relevant roadmap that will help you to best maximize your apps for success.*

- Habeebah Mazyck, Founder and President of Tafari, Inc.

*"I found the concepts in this book to be both a frank and fresh look at the disruptions facing small business owners right now, today, regarding their data and technology decisions combined with an easy-to-follow guide for embracing these changes with winning strategies and tactics."*

- Robert Hess, Digital Revenue & Data Leader in Adtech Industry

# CONTENTS

# THE BUSINESS APP
# REVOLUTION

Entrepreneur Sara Blakely, one of the richest women in the world, started her women's undergarments business in her small apartment in New York City. She had been selling fax machines for seven years when one day, after searching with no luck for a better-fitting pair of hose, she decided to create her own.

So at age 27, she launched Spanx, with $5,000 and a cell phone. Today, Spanx generates yearly revenues over $250 million. All it took was a few pieces of software, specifically business apps, and some incredible passion and focus. Blakely's use of technology is now a key strategy for many small business owners. Not too long ago, technology was mysterious magic that only the geeks knew their way around. The cloud, the smartphone, and business apps have changed everything.

Take the teacher who was able to build a strong online platform and become a social media influencer using nothing but her phone during her spare time. She eventually quit her day job and built a successful business with no tools other than her phone. It's fascinating that you can actually build a business this way. I certainly never considered the possibility of starting a business on a cell phone 20 years ago.

Or look at my own business, SquareStack, which you'll hear more about soon. Like many entrepreneurs, I started on a shoestring and a handful of business apps. I literally built our infrastructure on a number of inexpensive software as a service (SaaS) solutions and still, to this day, utilize every one of my original apps. In fact, today I subscribe to over 20 different business apps that have led the scaling of our business.

## Workplace Is Everyplace

The above examples offer a brief overview of the many advances in technology, what I call the emergence of the cloud. This is one of the most important developments in the tech world, impacting companies of all sizes. As a result of these advancements in tech tools, many large corporations now accept the fact that they don't need people in the office from 9:00 a.m. to 5:00 p.m. Additionally in the startup world, today's entrepreneur doesn't need to be "in the office" or "in the store" from 7:00 a.m. to 9:00 p.m. The idea here is that, especially in knowledge-based and professional services industries, you can work from anywhere, at any time. As a matter of fact, I'm writing this right now from a hotel lobby.

The idea that "a workplace is everyplace" is also very attractive to those who've either spent much of their career in an office. Now, mobility, flexibility, and working whenever and wherever you want are increasingly attractive incentives for many people to start their own businesses.

I often have this discussion with entrepreneurs and I have yet to find that most work more than 60 hours a week, at least in the early stages of their businesses. What's even more interesting is that being able to work anywhere enables entrepreneurs to spread their working hours out across a seven-day workweek. This allows these agile entrepreneurs to still raise a family and attain the balance they need to stay healthy and committed to the company they're building.

Today, terms like *lifestyle* business are commonplace. In the world of venture capital and tech startup executives, it's one of those code words, but it's one investors don't necessarily want to hear. It implies that these business owners aren't going to work around the clock. Don't get me wrong. There are plenty of reasonable, serious investors who don't feel this way and support their entrepreneurs fully. But do yourself a favor and, if possible, avoid using the term *lifestyle business* in the presence of investors!

But among entrepreneurs, it's heaven. It's the goal, right? You want to earn a healthy income, feel fulfilled in your business, and serve your customers, while also crafting a life where you're focused and connected to your family and friends. You don't need anyone to tell you how serious and committed you need to be to build and sustain a business. And how you choose to do that is your business.

It wasn't long ago that work was partitioned from our personal lives. Before the turn of the century you left work at work when you went home to your family and friends.

But when I was a kid, it started to change. I remember my mom complaining to my dad, "Stop bringing your work home!" Can you imagine that being said now? In today's world, *work is life and life is work*. They're blended so completely that it's second nature: take the call, walk the dog, write a report, book childcare, time for another cup of coffee.

Every week I have a conference call where there's at least one dog barking in the background. That's the beauty of the lifestyle entrepreneur. Working in one office every day throughout an entire career is becoming a thing of the past. As small business owners, we're moving constantly. To be sure, it's about working hard, but working when and wherever you want. I'm here to point out that to join the ranks of those living the mobile entrepreneurial lifestyle, you'll need the right technology.

For retail small business owners, you don't need to be reminded that it's probably the hardest industry to be in today. You've lived through the impact of Walmart, Target, and other mega-retailers. Additionally, many millennial entrepreneurs are launching ecommerce companies where they don't ever have to open a storefront at all. This is changing the world of retail dramatically. Those who remain brick-and-mortar players still need to develop a robust online presence—depending on their product category—if they aren't already there.

There are many retailers who are experiencing tremendous success with an online presence alone. In fact, there's now an official category called direct to consumer (DTC). DTC differs from the term B2C in a few respects. DTC companies, as the term implies, do sell to consumers;

and as such are technically a subset of the B2C umbrella. They differ in they have no physical retail or multi tiered distribution channels. Most successful DTC firms are seasoned, effective marketers who guide all their prospects to an online shopping experience. The DTC companies you have heard of include Harry's Razors, and Casper Beds. These nimble, innovative entrepreneurs are creating businesses that circumvent the physical retail channel. These technology-centric times require radical thinking where being a retailer doesn't mean signing a lease in a strip mall.

## *9.3% of retail economy DTC brands share in 2015*
SOURCE: US Census Bureau

But there's also a trend in the other direction. Take the men's shirt maker UntuckIt, for example. Here in Chicago, they recently opened a brick-and-mortar store on Michigan Avenue, although they started online. Then there's Google, which is now opening a store in Chicago's West Loop. I don't know if you'll be able to buy marketing at their front desk, but you'll certainly be able to buy their phones.

Online native companies will move to brick and mortar, while brick-and-mortar big companies have become durable businesses because they've also established an online presence. With the impacts of technology, legacy rituals like having to be in the office and punching a clock twice a day have disappeared in some industries. Certainly, there are still many industry segments where that's still the way of life, but most markets have witnessed this evolution and trend rapidly moving in.

Being an entrepreneur means working toward the Big Dream. The richness of your dream develops your drive to start a business. But it will actually be the planning, building, and implementation of your strategies and tactics that will make up the bulk of your journey. And it all starts today, with choosing and mastering technology that will enable you to succeed. Whether your business is service or product-based, you must make your company technology-centric.

Today, with the arrival and growth of cloud-based tools, along with the smartphone and the digital-first nature of the public, a solid technology infrastructure is essential for your business to compete effectively. I call this the *Appification Revolution of Business*. This revolution requires you as a business owner to take the best of the software you're already using, purchase complementary software in the form of apps, and then create an app ecosystem that will allow your customers to have the best buying experience.

The great news is that today, apps are inexpensive enough to let you compete with businesses much larger than yourself. This opportunity, in turn, translates into better profits with less effort. Whether you own a repair shop, sell crafts, or provide software solutions to manufacturing companies, as technology tools becomes less and less expensive, easier to use, and integrated into our everyday lives, the more critical it will be for you as an entrepreneur to keep pace.

Famous internet entrepreneur and venture capitalist Marc Andreessen is credited as saying, "Software is eating the world." At some point, I believe, all businesses will be technology based. Whether you walk dogs, run a food truck, or dole out psychotherapy, your customers will demand a way to engage with you via technology-driven tools. Additionally, your apps today can provide you with better and faster ways for your vendors and/or employees to work with you. This new opportunity will require you to integrate technology in the form of apps and an app suite into the very fabric of your business. In other words, it's time to *appify your business*.

I'm in the technology business, but I can vouch that many other entrepreneurs in my industry don't know how to leverage all the great technology now available to run their businesses. Since I'm fortunate enough to have worked in funded startups led by some very smart people, I made it my mission to deploy any relevant cloud-based software to run our enterprise. This conscious choice paid off in spades as I not only created great, agile solutions across our entire business, but it was truly cost effective. Whether it was an expense management solution or social media analytics, when I only had 10 employees or a hundred, these tools were central to our growth and success.

## *39% of small business owners work 60+ hours a week*

Today the technology revolution is still on fire. It's hard to catch one's breath with the amount of innovation being introduced. The emerging trend is that these innovations can now be used by small business owners just like you. In this book I'll guide you through the journey of learning how to take advantage of the cloud technology app revolution.

If you're not familiar with the term "business apps," they're a type of software that resides either on your desktop or laptop (called desktop apps) or your phone (referred to as mobile apps). When you open an app, it runs *inside* your device's operating system. It's independent of other apps, but can be integrated to work *together* with other apps (more on this later). Additionally, business apps are cloud-based or software as a service (SaaS) solutions that focus and enable specific work activities such as accounting, human resources tasks, social media posting, and the like.

In this book, I'll get you up to speed on how to purchase and grow a suite of business apps work to help you drive the success of your business.

## Your Current App Ownership

You're probably already using at least one app, if not many, for a variety of purposes, both business and personal. A business app is utilized solely for business purposes. For example, you may be using the ESPN app to get the latest scores for all your favorite sports teams, but you engage Salesforce for your business contact management activity. In other words, the term app has become standard jargon for all apps, no matter what their use. However, to differentiate between business and personal apps, I'll use the term business app to refer to all apps small business owners like yourself can use to run your business.

Business apps are growing quickly as the best technology tools to manage and scale businesses. I don't just mean that apps will save you time; they'll also deliver a myriad of measurable benefits. Figure 1 shows convincing research from the Local Search Association (www.lsa.org) and their Tech Adoption Index Survey that summarizes why small businesses love their business apps!

## FIGURE 1

**REASONS WHY SMBs HAVE SHIFTED TO OR ARE CONSIDERING CLOUD-BASED SERVICES**

| | HAVE SHIFTED | CONSIDERING |
|---|---|---|
| IT SAVES US TIME/ IS MORE EFFICIENT | 48% | 40% |
| IT COULD BE ACCESSED VIA SMARTPHONE APP | 29% | 23% |
| IT HAS MORE FEATURES AND CAPABILITIES THAN OUR OLD SERVICE | 29% | 23% |
| IT WAS SIMPLER OR EASIER TO USE | 26% | 28% |
| IT WAS LESS EXPENSIVE THAN OUR OLD SERVICE | 18% | 12% |

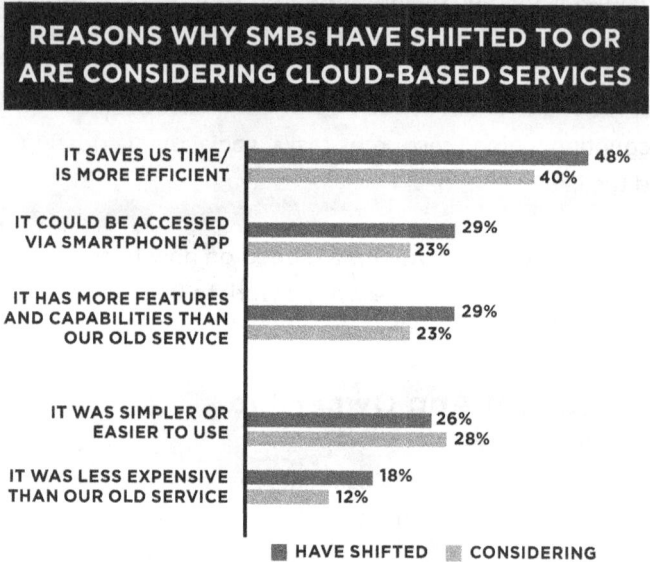

*Source: Local Search Association, Tech Adoption Index Survey, Wave III, October 2018*

There's no question that apps:

- Save you valuable time and money
- Enhance your brand.
- Connect you with your customers and employees everywhere
- Offer better, real-time connection to close your sales faster.[1]

## Time Is Your Greatest Asset

And as shared eloquently in a *Psychology Today* article:

"Time is more valuable than money. Most people look at their bank accounts with great attention and assess how much money they must spend, to invest, and to give away… … In fact, time is much more valuable than money because you can use your time to make money, but you can't use money to purchase more time."[2]

We all know that time is our most valuable commodity. Countless books, blogs, and television self-help evangelists have preached this long- trending message. Yet statistics show a different picture as to how poorly we currently optimize our time. According to the US Department of Labor, there's a real lack of productivity in our workplaces today. Why?

## *36% Small business owners time spent practicing their craft*

Source: LSA Tech Adoption Index Survey Wave II

The average American works 8.8 hours every day. According to a study of nearly 2,000 full-time office workers by the US Department of Labor, most people aren't working a good portion of the time they're at work. So what are they doing? The most popular unproductive activities listed are:

- Reading news websites—65 minutes
- Checking social media—44 minutes

- Discussing non-work-related things with co-workers—40 minutes
- Searching for new jobs—26 minutes
- Taking smoke breaks—23 minutes
- Making calls to partners or friends—18 minutes
- Making hot drinks—17 minutes
- Texting or instant messaging—14 minutes
- Eating snacks—8 minutes
- Making food in office—7 minutes

Looking at this list, here's how the above stats apply to my daily life. As a non-smoker, I save the 23 minutes not smoking, and since my business is doing okay, I save an additional 26 minutes by not needing to look for a new job. I grab two Starbucks a day, so I save another 10 minutes there. That gives me back an entire hour.

However, I'm guilty as charged on checking social media and the news. But that has to change. You get the picture. There's no doubt that I can do a number of things to become more productive. I also a*ppify my business*, which saves even more time. So, if you have some of the above bad habits where you waste time daily, you can make up for your transgressions by *appifying your own business*!

There's a hurdle we first need to address. While business apps are the new central platform for small businesses, with 3.8 million in the Google store alone, it's daunting to decide which are best for your company. And within this broad ecosystem there are likely a half million business-centric apps that small businesses can utilize. We've downloaded and used plenty of consumer-centric apps, in categories such as a travel, fitness, or gaming. There are also literally hundreds of thousands of business apps to help us be productive in our work. You can bet that as our business lives continue to integrate more into our personal lives, so too will business apps become a must-have business necessity and an essential part of business toolkits.

## *197 billion app downloads in 2017*
### Source: Statista 2017

Additionally, to give you a sense of just how immersed many of us are in using apps, check out this stat:

The average smartphone owner spends **2 hours and 15 minutes** a day using apps—the equivalent of one month a year. The average person has **60-90 apps** installed on their phone, using around 30 of them each month and launching 9 per day.[3]

Pew Center confirms this quickening trend in Figure 2 below. The mobile phone might as well be permanently attached to our person as over three quarters of Americans go online at least daily and a full one-quarter are almost constantly online. Time is precious and more of it is going to being online, whether you are at work or at home or in between.

## FIGURE 2

**ROUGHLY THREE-QUARTERS OF AMERICANS GO ONLINE AT LEAST DAILY**

| DAILY 77% | | LESS THAN DAILY 11% | | |
|---|---|---|---|---|
| 26 | 43 | 8 | 6 | 5 |
| Almost Constantly | Several times a day | About once a day | Several times a week | Less often |

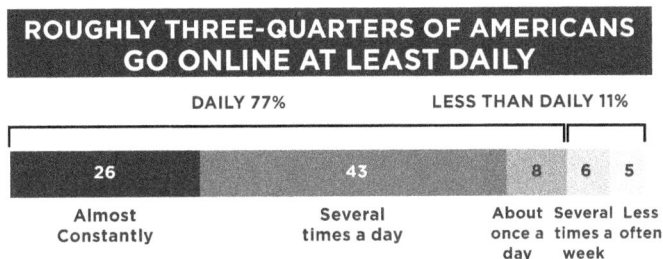

Note: Figures do not add up to 100% because non-internet users were not asked the question. Source: Survey conducted 3-10, 2018.

Let's take a closer look at the app revolution and how you can become one of its leaders.

## Simple Action Steps to Take Now

Conduct a time audit of your typical day. From the moment you wake to heading to bed. Pay extra attention to how work and personal time are intertwined through the course of the day

Spend some time reviewing your smartphone apps. How many are for personal use v. business use. Do the same with your laptop and desktop.

Be sure to review recent research studies on how we spend our time everyday. Our federal government's Bureau of Labor Statistics actually collects comprehensive data on time use, which you can view here:

http://www.pewinternet.org/
https://www.bls.gov/tus/

# THE APPSTACK AS YOUR OPERATING SYSTEM

There are hundreds of stories about how small businesses used simple apps to explode their business growth. A great example is food trucks that strategically use Twitter to broadcast their locations for the day, along with their unique menus and daily specials. Now thousands of food businesses like Panera and Starbucks use apps for placing orders with no wait time, just a quick pickup at a side counter location once you arrive.

There's no question that the business app revolution is well underway. These apps can do many things, with their main focus on helping you maintain and run your business. But beyond this, business apps can also help you become a disruptor and dominate your industry. It all depends on the apps, your business, and how creative you want to be.

One of my favorite review sites is G2, which is based in Chicago, where my company and I reside. Take a look at their website: www.g2crowd.com. They've reviewed thousands of software applications that apply only to business use, with 30-plus categories that include payroll, HR, project management, programmatic media, social media, and operations. As you can see, the world of business software is growing by leaps and bounds, and you need to understand what's going on with them.

Innovation in cloud-based software is being fueled by venture capital as well as out of the pockets of bright, passionate entrepreneurs who see business apps as tools to provide solutions for problems. Your goal in this world of appification will be to figure out what you actually need and who is producing the best solutions to meet those needs. I'll cover this topic later in the book.

As new industries grow, their collective participants will continue to evolve the definition of the app ecosystem. There are better and faster ways of finding and deploying apps in your business. Rather than buying a software license and installing it on your servers or computers, which adds the further challenge of keeping up with new versions, you can simply go online and sign up for an app (software service) in minutes and start using it immediately. Typically you pay a monthly fee, thereby eliminating costly licensing contracts.

*74% use 1+ app*
*27% use 5+ apps*
*small business app usage*
Source: Salesforce SMB Report 2018

Innovative developers are seeing opportunity in the challenges of specific business problems. They're creating new apps to solve the variety of market problems that are constantly emerging. And recently, small business owners are actively developing their own apps. They mostly target customers and charge full steam ahead into innovative channels to reach and engage their customers on platforms they prefer.

Figure 3 summarizes how many apps are being created by category. It's no great surprise that gaming, entertainment, and travel top the list. But there's a business just behind them at number four. And several categories, like travel, food, and drink, also have distinct business-driven purposes.

## FIGURE 3

| Category | Percentage |
|---|---|
| GAMES | 24.86% |
| BUSINESS | 9.77% |
| EDUCATION | 8.5% |
| LIFESTYLE | 8.32% |
| ENTERTAINMENT | 6.03% |
| UTILITIES | 5.06% |
| TRAVEL | 3.9% |
| HEALTH & FITNESS | 3.01% |
| BOOK | 2.92% |
| FOOD & DRINK | 2.89% |
| PRODUCTIVITY | 2.66% |
| MUSIC | 2.48% |
| FINANCE | 2.27% |

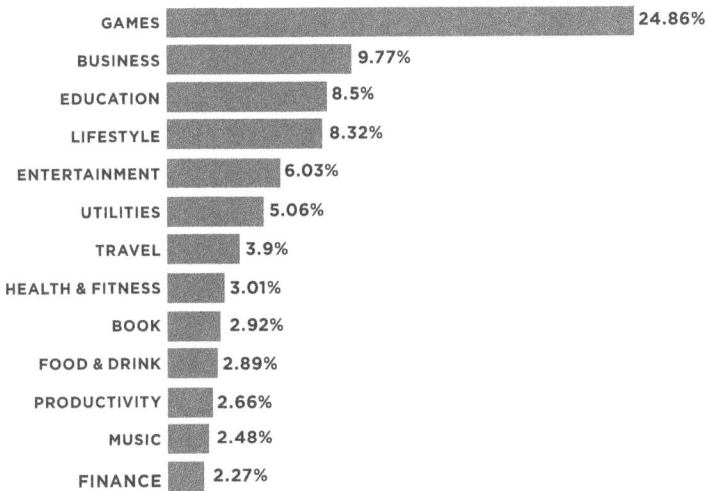

Source: Stasista.com, October 2018

## How Can Apps Help Your Business?

For any task you have to take on in your business, there's an app for it. Look at it this way: for every silo of your business enterprise, there's the underlying work activity. And the ultimate goal of a software developer is to deliver a solution that helps you get things done faster, better, and cheaper.

Consider the following trends, which illuminate why you should embrace the power of business apps:

- The amount of time people spend on mobile devices alone has increased by 575% in the last three years.
- 80% of this time was spent using apps.
- Apps offer substantially better connection, interaction, and responses from customers than traditional websites.[4]

There's no question that apps should now be the operating control center of your business. This is true whether you're a solopreneur or a fast-growth small to mid-sized company.

When you're looking at business apps, think about your entire enterprise, not just one silo or function. Here are the some of the major categories where business apps deliver on their promise to make your work more efficient:

Business intelligence and analytics
Collaboration
Customer relationship management
Ecommerce
Financial services
Human resources
Inventory control
Industry utility (salon, auto, grocery)
Operations and infrastructure
Productivity and project management
Recruiting and outsourcing
Social media management

There isn't a single activity in your business that is not

being addressed with a relevant business app. Within each general department, you'll find a level of specialization that continues to proliferate. For instance, just in financial services alone, there are a few dozen subcategories of apps such as expense management, cash flow, invoicing, and loan management.

## Appifying Your Business

I get pretty excited and start to babble passionately about the power and glory of APPS, in CAPS! I often say, "There's an app for that!"

Because business apps are the new essential tech tools for optimal business growth, I created the concept of *appifying your business*. Having worked in the media and marketing technology industries, talking to many vendors and small business users, it became clear to me that small business owners would need help choosing which apps would help them grow their businesses faster and better. Ideas by themselves without smart execution won't deliver results. *Appifying your business* offers you a simple yet powerful process to achieve and sustain success.

## *48% save time shifting to the cloud*

Source: LSA.Org Tech Adoption Survey Wave III

In this book you'll note terms like *appify, appification, app-ready, AppStack*, and their derivatives used throughout. Fear not, as these terms will become second nature, and you'll embrace technology like never before. Let's now dig into how you'll use these terms, and what they actually mean from an execution standpoint.

## Not Your Father's Internet

In the last chapter I indicated that for our purposes, a business app is any software, or *digitally based business solution*, that you use in the process of getting work done. Of course, you can use software like QuickBooks at home, but in the entrepreneurial world, it's the core *financial software* you use to run your business. Also, while you can use it on your mobile phone, most of us do the heavy lifting with Intuit on our laptop or desktop. But I'll still call it a business app.

So, for example, you may have an Expedia account that you also use as a consumer, but going forward, let's call it a business app. I don't know about you, but my Expedia account is absolutely overworked for all my business trips. Once in a while, though, I'll sneak in a weekend jaunt with my wife and actually book via Expedia, but using my personal rather than my business Visa card. Make sense?

Also, and this is an important distinction, I'm calling a simple web interface to a business vendor a business app. Why? Because you're probably moving from an analog method (phone, fax, live sales call) to digital engagement (order supplies, check on the status of a project, deposit a check) with your vendor or partner.

Then there's your website. That's not a pure app as defined earlier, but it's definitely a major player for conducting your business online. This is critical to remember as I talk later in the book about vertical apps, such as salon, automotive, and legal software and the like. Suffice it to say, if you're engaging via a web channel on your phone, laptop, or desktop, I'll also call those channels business apps.

Anything connected to and working by means of an IT interface I'll also characterize as a business app. You've probably noticed that many of your vendors have expressly required you to engage with them online. This is all about saving them money as much as it's about their own internal advances to get up to speed. While mostly mid-sized to large companies have deployed these services online, now smaller companies are starting to operate exclusively online. Just as we're talking about *appifying your business*, you can bet many others are, too, including your vendors.

## The AppStack as a Company Asset

You should view your own technology as your AppStack, the aggregate of all your software and digitally based solutions. *It's the single most important operational platform needed to create and run a successful business.* No longer will your software be just another painful but necessary cost or a nuisance that you have to tend to every other day. Instead, your apps will now be as important as the electronic devices you run them on.

Your AppStack will hold your set of apps, which, once combined in an integrated group, will help you perform your daily, monthly, and yearly business tasks in as few steps as possible. Your AppStack will also provide your business with an integrated work environment, whereas a legacy software stack offers only minimum interaction with your software.

Note that your AppStack is a key asset in your business. As you become more proficient in enabling and tracking all the key data within your enterprise, you'll realize that your data is another valuable asset you own, like your inventory, customer list, real estate, and brand value. Don't underestimate its power. You must value your data as a key asset. Extracting informative insights from it ranks alongside tracking your cash flow and listening to your customer as must-do's in today's environment.

That's why more and more businesses are looking at the creation or improvement of the AppStack as their centralized, powerful engine, necessary to sustaining success. If you tend to your AppStacks as you do other parts of your business you'll be better able to plan for growth. Additionally, if you ever want to sell your business, you can bet potential buyers will want to know what sort of technology stack you have and what sort of data you own, especially around customer acquisition and growth.

While businesses for whom technology is not a priority are still being bought and sold, the revolution is underway, and they're becoming less common. As cloud technology continues to innovate and become ubiquitous, inquiries into your AppStack will be as routine as asking what your inventory looks like.

If you're like other small business owners, what's driving you to embrace technology is pressure from many of your vendors and commercial partners. Your payroll processor, bank, and other product suppliers are all focused on digitizing their customer relationships. They now require you to order and inquire via their web portals or business apps. The days of actually faxing an order, speaking to a customer service representative, or meeting a sales rep in person are almost all distant memories. It's routine business as efficiency, speed, and the underlying data collected in all digital transactions provide obvious benefits for both parties.

## *$175.8 billion in 2018 total spend on public cloud computing market*

Source: Gartner 2018

I don't need to tell you, being a diehard who insists on doing business the old-fashioned way is really inefficient. Besides, if you do hold out from sheer stubbornness, you might not find anyone to do business with! The millennial generation prefers to do business via a keyboard, primarily on a smartphone. The youngest portion of that demographic likely never did business the old-fashioned way. According to recent research from Local Search Association, here's a snapshot of how age matters in terms of smartphone usage:

- 18–34      56% By phone
- 35–54      43% By phone
- 55–64      24% By phone
- 65+        19% By phone

Recently, I was head of business development for an ad-tech company where we had many millennial sales executives who in turn, worked with many millennial buyers. We often closed fairly large deals without a live word spoken between the parties. This may sound pretty outrageous to most baby boomers, but indeed, millennial work transactions are leaning into a pure digital occurrence. It happens via text, email, Google Chat, DocuSign, and a DM to boot. You'd better get used to it. You really have little choice but to *appify your business*.

## Innovate or Die

Innovation is a loaded term. As a mentor at some of Chicago's tech incubators, I can vouch for how this word is bandied about almost carelessly. It's the sound byte of the era. And while it's surely an aspiration for all, it certainly isn't so easily executed. From Fortune 500 firms to the small start-up ecosystem, everybody is an innovator. How is that possible? Is it a mirage, or can a small retailer or two-man law firm innovate? The answer is, "Hell, yes!"

Innovation doesn't have to come in the form of new services or products, or a new way to hire and nurture employees. Of course, it can, but if you really want to prioritize innovation, start by *appifying* your business. This involves investing in foundational systems that will make your business hum. This is innovation that is tangible, measurable, and scalable. And although it's not glamorous work and is, no doubt, outside your comfort zone, it will pay off in spades.

I sheepishly confess I was not very tech savvy through the early years of my career. As a young boomer in the 1980s, we made calls on a landline, faxed orders, and had inboxes filled with little pink message notes. Through the 1990s I witnessed the rapid adoption of email and the nascent emergence of Web 1.0. Technology was still a scary experience for most business executives. I spent a decade working for Chicago-based media company, Crain Communications. I had the additional good fortune of working for leading marketing business journal, *Advertising Age*. There, I had a front row seat for Web 1.0 and experienced and survived the irrational exuberance of the era, as Alan Greenspan once noted.

Interestingly, most business executives viewed technology in those early days as a mysterious and intimidating entity. It was a fairly widely held belief that only a few oddball nerds knew how to actually make it work. But by the 1980s and certainly into the 1990s, technology evolved into the terrain of a chosen few. At that time, most small and mid-sized businesses knew they needed tech, but they completely and uncompromisingly deferred to "the experts." Even those internet entrepreneurs *who were creating the web didn't know how to deploy technology for their own startups.*

As I'll discuss later in the book, things have completely changed since then. The internet, the cloud, and the apps on our smartphones have totally reengineered how we as consumers and business owners engage tech. It's now a personal experience.

Today, the cloud is another fundamental asset of your business. Now that your vendors, customers, and millennial employees are well-entrenched in using smartphones and countless business apps as a routine part of their workday, you have no choice but to do so yourself.

Yet instead of looking at this through a reactive lens, realize that the cloud supports business improvement and growth. New business apps cover the gamut enabling business transformation, from improving client engagement and insights to empowering employees and helping you run more efficient operations. These are real opportunities, but at the same time, can be overwhelming. That's where *appifying your business* will indeed help you.

Also, realize that technology is a primary reason that Fortune 500 companies are leading the way, and, in many cases, crushing the small business ecosystem. Witness what has happened to Main Street in the last few decades. Here, the reasons include the ability of behemoth companies like Walmart and Amazon to scale and grow on the backs of Main Street. In the process, you can bet the cloud empowered their success. Amazon itself owns Amazon Web Services (AWS) that, as a separate subsidiary, is itself a gigantic business. For example, in the first quarter of 2018, Amazon Web Services reported sales of $5.44 billion, up 50% from 2017, and now it constitutes 11% of Amazon's revenue.

## *50% of all Amazon.com sales from small businesses*

Source: Amazon 2018

Not coincidentally, AWS is powering a great part of the appification of business, being a default choice for small and larger businesses to manage their technology in the cloud. The counterintuitive trend is that AWS is also allowing small businesses to actually compete at fair prices, and with the same toolkits that Fortune 500 companies leverage. Here as a small business, if you choose, you can benefit by making a personal commitment to replicate in your business the toolkit that will let you grow like the big companies. All those other commitments you make to be the best mean nothing if you don't have the chops to build and scale your AppStack. Case closed.

Before I move on, let's summarize what I've presented so far. As consumers, we're all regularly using apps to do all sorts of activities. Now our business lives are becoming appified. The cloud is driving business activity and productivity at breakneck speed. Therefore, today small business owners have to be committed to this revolution or become a casualty. While many of us still have the misguided perception that technology is too hard to learn, the cloud has also changed this dynamic. All business apps are designed for the layperson or technology-challenged executive.

Next let's now take a look at what technology you likely already own, if not use, routinely. We'll also look at the typical suite of apps that can make your business run efficiently and effectively.

## Simple Action Steps to Take Now

Conduct a time audit of a full weekday from waking up to heading to bed. See just how you're using your time, down to the minute. Measure your work and personal time and what you define as mundane versus productive time.

- Check out your smartphone's internal data tools to turn on how you're using your data and time on all your apps.

- Read one of the small business studies on technology available at these companies' websites:
    Salesforce
    G2 Crowd
    Smallbiztrends

# THE STANDARD ISSUE APPSTACK: WHAT APPS DO I NEED?

Now that we've discussed the technology landscape and why business apps have become so popular, let's talk about how your own business apps can work together to create an *optimized* system. You probably already use a few apps, but haven't realized the power of having an organized technology suite of business apps. When operating in unison, this suite runs a well-honed machine that powers your business at its core.

Have you heard the term *tech stack*, by chance? Most early adopters of technology, technology services vendors, or new entrepreneurs with corporate work pedigrees likely have. In the last few years, the term has trickled down to many small business owners. The cloud revolution has allowed the creation and scaling of every business's tech stack. Business app, as another term gaining traction, guides me to rename the tech stack to a more relevant parlance, the AppStack.

A standard AppStack can comprise business apps in:

• Banking
• Facebook

- Google
- QuickBooks
- Salesforce
- Twitter
- And many more

As for my own business, SquareStack, I deploy a more than 35 business apps, and another half dozen industry media and research apps. They fall into the following top-level categories:

- SaaS-based software: as a reminder, any software that you're paying a fee for that you manage activities via a self-service portal
- All vendor-provided software or web-based portals to manage and administrate your business
- Any business relevant website, app, or link to a public online portal that helps a small business owner do their job

In my stack, I have expense management software, Concur, customer relationship management (CRM) Solution, Crisp Chat, marketing software, Adobe Creative Suite, portals like Business.com and Expedia for content and travel respectively, and, finally, all my bank and credit-line password-protected admin sites.

## *73% of all businesses say they will run primarily on SaaS/apps by 2020*

SOURCE: BetterCloud State of Cloud Marketplace 2018

I talk to many small business owners and it amazes me that many don't realize they already have a rudimentary AppStack in place. They also don't realize that they're already investing a decent amount of money in software and managing many of their routine activities via their AppStack. Nothing is more fulfilling than helping entrepreneurs realize that right under their noses they have the foundation for a thriving, scalable technology infrastructure.

## Your AppStack Checklist

Start sizing up your AppStack by writing down what software, websites, and vendor apps you use everyday in the following categories:

Advertising_____

Ecommerce_____

Email_____

Financial (bank, credit)_____

Human resources_____

Industry specific_____

Payroll_____

Procurement_____

Project management_____

Recruitment_____

Social media_____

Website analytics_____

If you're like the average small business owner, you can probably claim a minimum of a half dozen of these, whether they're free website portals or paid software. They individually help you orchestrate your workday and will only grow more important over time. Again, with 500,000 apps currently in the small to mid-sized business ecosystem, with innovation they will continue to grow unabated. This revolution will no doubt bring with it further efficiencies and innovations, along with some new challenges.

## What Your Peers Are Doing

The entire small business community has embraced the cloud across the entire business infrastructure and as Figure 4 summarizes, increasingly technology is impacting all parts of the business. And not surprisingly, the commitment continues to grow.

## FIGURE 4

CLOUD-BASED TECHNOLOGY ADOPTION

**TIMING OF SHIFT**

| 33% | 33% | 22% | 12% |
|-----|-----|-----|-----|
| Within 6 months | 6 to 12 Months | 1-2 Years | > 2 Years |

SOURCE: Local Search Association, Tech Adoption Index Survey, Wave III, October 2018

## New App Challenges

With growth comes growing pains. For example, you'll find yourself constantly bombarded with one better-looking new app offer after another. How will you know what apps are really the best for you and which just have a lot of strong marketing dollars behind them?

Many of these app-makers are funded early-stage firms and many won't make it. I can vouch for this, having come from this world: there's nothing more frustrating and time-consuming than picking the wrong business app.

If you're already using business apps, you're probably not using them to their fullest capabilities. Don't despair. Even those of us who've committed to leveraging these great tools are still learning and working our way to greater efficiency. When you picked up this book, you already made an additional investment of time to learn how to grow an AppStack more effectively. Going forward, I'll share additional stories about how other small business owners and entrepreneurs are using and building their business app proficiency, and what this is doing for their business.

Before you hyperventilate over which apps to use, know that there are many resources to help you make the right decisions. Researching the small business technology landscape and how many business software review sites categorize the ecosystem, I can safely estimate that there are 25+ categories that will about cover all the function and subsequent relevant business apps that a small business can utilize. Here they are in Figure 5:

## Figure 5

| | | |
|---|---|---|
| UNCATEGORIZED | ACCOUNTING & FINANCE | AUTOMOTIVE SOFTWARE |
| COLLABORATION | COMMUNICATIONS | EMAIL |
| INFORMATION TECHNOLOGY | LEGAL & OPERATIONS | MARKETING & ADVERTISING |

SOURCE: SquareStack, December 2018

There are media, online directories, trade shows, salespeople, and technology staffers and consultants at the ready to help marketing teams across companies of all sizes. Companies like Cisco, Intuit, Oracle, and Zoho, to name a few, also help take the pain out of the tech integration process by bundling a number of business apps together, thereby making selection easier.

*18% shifted to CRM in the cloud*
*16% plan to shift to CRM in the cloud*

SOURCE: LSA.org Tech Adoption Index Wave III 2018

Let's take a look at one of the categories and how many different business apps populate the function. Let's take a look at another general category, CRM. You may have made the leap and activated a CRM solution. I am sure that decision-making process was a tedious and confusing journey. The reality is that even the largest companies are still trying to figure out how to optimize the investment, and how it will integrate into current systems. Most of us, including corporate types, still have no idea what the inherent return on investment is or will be. Here is a sample of the myriad of CRM choices there are for the small business owner, as outlined in Figure 6.

## FIGURE 6

**CRM + DEMAND GENERATION BUSINESS APPS**

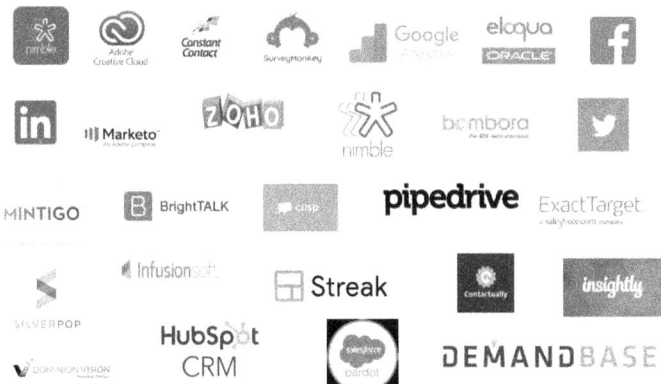

SOURCE: www.fitsmallbusiness.com, October 2018

Whatever the specific function, in any size company in search of a solution for any variety of challenges, there will constantly be new software solutions coming onto the market to solve them. There's simply no looking back.

And what about us small business owners? Research shows that many of us do not have an on-staff IT director, or maybe not even a part-time one, at that. Beyond the obvious challenges that creates, you're most likely being bombarded by vendors all day long. They're coming at you on the web, knocking at your door, and more frequently by traditional advertising (radio, TV, outdoor), all clamoring for you to buy the best software on earth: theirs!

Again, my goal with this book is to give you the resources you need to adapt to this new AI landscape and help you make wise decisions.

## The Small Business Landscape

The business app landscape is well on its way to being an expansive ecosystem, comprising many business categories and subsequent software solutions. The following will simplify it as much as possible and prepare you to focus on what you need and when

I will follow the same design and structure as the other technology category infographics I shared earlier. And I'll take some license and call it the Small Business Appiscape. A few comments before we digest the detail:

I've followed the industry's best practices and definitions on software categories. These specific disciplines are familiar to you, and these generic category levels are fairly standard for how I view and operate our businesses.

- I could dive deeper into each category with subsets, but for this exercise, I'll keep my explanations at a higher "departmental" level.
- I'm not including all or even a majority of the business app companies that provide services in the designated categories. In our Appendix in References and Resources, you will find a list of these valuable review sites and their URLs.
- The primary takeaway is to understand that you must own and operate your very own AppStack. Even as a small company, you need a robust technology enterprise that, in turn, you must manage, assess, and optimize for the good of your business. Tending to it must be as routine as reviewing your bank statement, checking inventory, and the daily team meeting. These are the table stakes in today's small business environment.

In many respects, the small business AppStack is no less complex or important than that of a Fortune 500 company. But there are key points of distinction:

- All of the small business apps are less expensive but no less robust in terms of capabilities than corporate-sized solutions.
- Many small business app-makers have taken into account the lack of an IT director on staff. Subsequently they make software more user-friendly, so any layperson or generalist can use it effectively. This is really important to know, as the revolution of business apps is all about user experience. User experience (UX) is at the heart of all new software innovation. As the software use explodes, consumers and business executives will be utilizing

- more software to power their working and personal lifestyles. So it's critical that the software is intuitive, easy to use, and affordable.
- Thousands of hours are invested in user-experience testing and many design iterations of the software are cycled before it even sees the light of day to paying customers.

## Business App Composition

I've shared the larger ecosystem of business apps, categories, and definitions. Let's take a look at what a fairly standard AppStack looks like for the small business owner. The following categories capture most of  the activities inherent in running a business. All that I do—from functions to employee engagement—will likely be assignable to one of these categories:

Accounting and finance
Business intelligence and analytics
Collaboration
Communications
Customer relationship management
Design and production
Email
Human resources and employee relations
Information technology
Legal
Marketing and advertising
Productivity and project management
Recruiting and outsourcing
Retail and ecommerce
Sales

Security
Shopping
Social media management
Startup planning
Travel and hospitality
Website development and management

As a fellow small business owner, I'd like to share my own AppStack. By no means are we done. I don't think we'll ever be done, but, as I mentioned, we currently have 35+ apps that power our enterprise. I can say with confidence that I'd be lost without this powerful suite of apps. It's helped us achieve exciting growth while also enabling our proactive strategic decision making. Here in Figure 7, I summarize my own AppStack.

## FIGURE 7

My Own AppStack

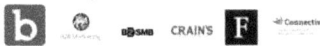

SOURCE: SquareStack.com, December 2018

## A Day in the Life of an Entrepreneur Using an AppStack

What I'm about to share with you will likely make a lot of sense, but it may also surprise you just how much technology you already use. Following is an overview of my daily ritual driven by technology, and the great variety of business apps that help run my business:

- **Morning coffee:** I start my morning with the essential cup of coffee in hand, fire up the laptop, and take a first look through my financial, social, and vertical industry apps. As a fellow small business owner, I have to check my bank account first, followed by my other line of credit, and credit card accounts. While I usually remember my general cash-on-hand amount from week to week, it's also critical to know if any payments or credits have come in and what checks have cleared. In the early days of our startup, we were juggling cash flow on an almost daily basis.

- Also, I now have an easier navigational process to manage any cash or credit transfers, toggling between business apps and screens to execute what I need to sustain or scale my business, daily financials, and investments. For those of you who have financial executives on your team at least part-time, you can always delegate those decisions at an execution level, but nothing beats seeing the numbers in real time on your screen.

- **Social media:** The next thing I usually check is our social media stats. SquareStack is primarily a business-to-business (B2B) model, and I do a lot of posting on LinkedIn and Twitter to reach our target decisionmakers. My team posts content to our other social pages weekly, and we have a rigorous marketing funnel to track those interested in our services. Additionally, since we're targeting other businesses, we rely less on the consumer-centric social platforms like Facebook, Instagram, and Pinterest. (However, you'd be pleasantly surprised how effective B2B advertising is on Facebook!)

A daily check of our metrics is, again, a habit that I didn't have a year ago, but it's now a routine activity for me. It's also important to review your stats daily. Often, I don't feel moved by our business-building activities since I'm entrenched in the daily drudgery of running it. Becoming connected to your data on a routine basis absolutely changes your mindset.

- **Business apps:** After I've checked our social media stats, I turn my attention to some of the business apps that are more directly related to the industry I'm in, technology. While my development guys are working with tech tools like Drupal, Plaid, and Amazon Web Services, I, too, as the leader, have access to their systems. This allows me to track the progress of their projects, post comments, and confirm for them that I'm involved—but not overly so—and encourage their good work. Again, a little bit of access to the functional activities of your business goes a long way toward building your own confidence in what the team is doing and why you're paying them what you do.

- **Infrastructure software and vendor portals:** Another activity I find helpful and necessary to my morning business routine is accessing our infrastructure software and vendor portals. SquareStack is still a small business, and while I have development guys and gals working for me, I don't technically have a COO or CIO. So I personally manage all of our general and administrative (G&A) expenses activity with my finance director. I also manage or check into our HR, expense management, real estate, recruitment, payroll, travel, and project management tools. I decide whether to check what our payment plan is or the level of service I signed on for, and sometimes want to just learn more about the filtering tools within the software. A few minutes dabbling here and there can go a long way.

  This bears some further discussion. As I said earlier, our company deploys 35+ business apps. I don't often dive deeply into each business app's robust capabilities. This is a fairly common confession by many of my peers. So don't feel too overwhelmed around the lack of depth you're achieving in terms of using your apps' metrics and filters. Master the global view first. Then, as you build confidence and routine, start to allocate more time to diving deeper into the data, and leveraging the many filters each business app offers. Another suggestion would be to delegate responsibility to your team on the analysis of the data resident in each app. If anything, this will empower them to feel more engaged their area of responsibility in the business.

# *25+ business app categories 500,000+ business apps*

Source: SquareStack 2018

- **Business travel:** One last area I'll share about my daily AppStack visit is around business travel. SquareStack's commercial partners are association, business media, and franchiser companies based all over the country. Since we have one business development executive charged with nurturing and developing new partners, most of which are located in New York, Washington, San Francisco, and in the Midwest, you can bet we use our travel business apps often and manage our spending diligently.

  Our company uses Hotel Tonight, Expedia, Gogo Inflight, and a host of conference call services. Concur helps us manage all our expenses. Don't underestimate the need for such business apps if your company requires travel. I'm sure that many of you are currently using these business apps. These are just as much a part of your AppStack as any other more obviously business-oriented app.

The above should have provided you with a clear view of my business app usage. I use several other business apps, but I'll save discussion of those for later.

## What Does This Mean for You?

Long term, as a business owner, there are significant reasons to build your own AppStack. Designate the handful of apps you're already using as your company's official technology platform. You'll soon discover how much time and money you'll save in the long run, and how engaged you'll become in tracking the company's metrics in real time. After the initial investment of moving to a more app-centric work ritual, you'll wonder what took you so long. According to Rackspace's State of Cloud Adoption Report,[5] the benefits of activating business apps are profound:

- 51% say they reduce time spent managing IT
- 50% say they require fewer internal IT resources
- 94% say they have produced security benefits
- 75% say they have improved Service availability
- 96% say they have less worry on outages


And the time and money savings are evident:
- 50% say they can pursue new opportunities because of the time saved managing via the cloud
- 70% have reinvested money saved as a result of moving to the cloud


If you're a small business retailer who feels the heat from Amazon, Walmart, Starbucks, and Alibaba, business apps can be your competitive toolkit to sustain and build your business.

The Local Search Association asked small business retailers about this trend and here's what they learned:

- 68% believe that national brands have marketing and tech tools at their disposal that they do not.
- 27% believe that competition from national chains and large enterprises is more intense than before.

- 7% believe that competition from national chains and large enterprises is less intense than before.

The case for having a more robust, or "full" AppStack, is clearly made here, and the research confirms this. They asked their small business database about the number of apps they use. They found that the more these apps (specifically marketing and sales apps) are deployed across the various silos of their businesses, the greater the increase of their customer base and the decrease of lost business.

More data will soon emerge that supports the above finding. Later in this book I'll share some anecdotal stories from business owners who have increased their business by building more robust AppStacks.

As I've said, the way we work as small business owners has dramatically changed. We can work more independently and in a more agile manner. Speed and iteration matter and the cloud-based AppStack is now the nervous system for this new work ritual. Solutions that aren't mobile and cloud-based first will quickly fail.

Sales and marketing have completely and fundamentally changed. As our business-to-business or consumer-facing markets become more mobile-oriented, and the physical-engagement experience of buying a product or service becomes less necessary, we've found we need to become even more *customer-centric*. We have no choice but to embrace the cloud. Remember, not just your buyers, but your workers and vendors, too, are moving to cloud-based communication and commerce.

So where do you go from here? In the next chapter, I'll discuss all the benefits and new resources that will help you grow exponentially as you begin to add them into your AppStack, always realizing that you must commit to work with it daily, as it's the foundation of your business.

Let's look at how you can proceed to build your own AppStack focusing on the essential parts of your enterprise.

## The Appify Your Business App Playbook Checklist

The following checklist is your essential guide to *appifying* your business. It will show you where you stand today with your technology enterprise, what you need to prioritize over the next few months, and what changes you need to make with your current technology. Afterward, complete the Playbook Checklist. This will show you where you are in terms of adoption and knowledge on the Cloud-based technology curve.

## Financial Enterprise

It's all about the money, the margin. The financial function is the best place to start your AppStack. You save time here and will save money. Start by making sure you're completely connected to your bank, credit cards, and lines of credit via their SaaS and mobile applications.

Investigate, research, and add to your business AppStack smartly in areas like expense management, vendor payment systems, shipping and postage, and ecommerce.

## Data Security

This is still the number-one technology small businesses need to take a serious look at in today's world of malware and breaches. There are also significant changes that have come about in Europe now with general data protection regulation (GDPR). I also see there's some lack of concern with many small business owners who feel they're too small or insignificant to worry about these new regulations in Europe. Not so. No matter the size of your firm, the number of clients you have, or the number of systems you have, your website and all apps need to be protected by the best in security software.

Lean first into your vendors for assurances and explanations on their firewalls and commitment to guarding your data. AWS, ADP, Microsoft, and many of the business app-makers are focused on this initiative for all their clients, no matter their size.

## Email Marketing

Build a database, and then what? Market to them, of course! And do it with smart frequency. There are many good business apps that will drive your campaigns, and several are connected to the next two required marketing systems to provide you a troika of powerful tools to build your customer base and upsell current ones.

## Customer Relationship Management (CRM)

Depending on what research you refer to, it's safe to say that more than half of all small business owners have made the leap to turning on a CRM solution. It's obvious to most small business owners that this business app is essential to scaling their insights into customer behavior, marketing effectiveness, and investments across the enterprise. I believe that this is the major inflection point where, once committed to CRM, small business owners are well on their way to *appifying* their business.

## Marketing Automation (MA)

This is the last of the marketing trio apps, and for many, the last one to wrap one's head around. Going hand in hand with CRM, this app is more about your inbound marketing activity than what your outbound messaging generates. A basic objective of MA business apps is to score leads, segment messages, and set up processes that will activate specialized messages that tune into and are on target as to where that prospect or customer is in their buying journey.

## Mobile "Ubiquity"

Lots to cover here, but broadly speaking, small businesses see mobile as affecting everything in the enterprise. The checklist includes making sure your website is mobile-ready as well as creating your own app that customers can use. It also includes activating mobile payment systems specifically if you're business-to-consumer (B2C) focused—and be sure that your outbound marketing commits to a mobile-centric strategy.

*Top 5 Business Apps*
*1-10 Employee Companies*
*GSuite*
*GitHub*
*AWS*
*Slack*
*MailChimp*

Source: B2SMB Institute/ Blissfully 2018

## Human Resources Software

This was one of the other technologies that over half of small business owners have committed to. HR business apps can automate so much of the tedious detail of administrative functions, including benefits, time off, and company policies. Insurance companies also are providing smart app solutions for you to manage employees and policies, and offer them self-service. It's also a good idea to look for some strategic options like tracking long-term employee development and continuing online education.

## Website Implementation and Enhancement Tools

Even if you don't have an online presence right now, you can make the leap with little pain. Companies like GoDaddy, SquareSpace, and Microsoft offer SaaS-based apps so that most laymen can create a decent looking website. Many B2C small businesses have also decided to let Facebook serve as their default website. In B2B, it's practically a requirement to have a functional website if you want to be taken seriously by future and current customers.

## Chat X 2: Chatbots and Chat Function

There's a whole lot going on in this segment, but consider an investment here. With the recent upsurge in the popularity of messaging apps, this is an area to continually look into. Many website owners have reduced their Customer service costs by using these business apps for real time customer guidance.

## Internal Collaboration Tools

For small business owners who have more than a handful of employees and certainly ones scaling quickly, the move to collaboration apps is essential. In the old days, collaboration was a face-to-face activity. With the increasing availability of business app collaborative tools, it's no longer necessary to spend so much capital for the live in-person meeting. Many apps are enabling videoconferencing, internal team chat, iterative project management platforms, and more.

How much more frustration can your team take with that endless email chain? Tools like Slack, Trello, and GoToMeeting are leading this more active segment of business apps.

## Vendor App Engagement

This is pretty straightforward. Embrace your vendors and activate their business apps when you can. Here, specifically I mean your traditional vendors and suppliers. Whether it's your salon supplies partner or your local FedEx store, each of these vendors sees the future and is building online access to simplify your engagement with them (and, of course, to cut their costs and build their own internal efficiencies).

## Master Dashboarding

Monitor the expansive and critical data sets that emerge from all your business apps. Your data is a valuable company asset, and one that you can't let sit without engagement. Every day, everyone should bookmark all the dashboards of real-time data that each app generates. Check your QuickBooks dashboard: did that deposit come in? Check your website analytics: is that new social campaign bringing people to the site? Check your supplier portal: is the product en route yet? Imagine making several phone calls or sending a few emails versus driving to the bank. Huh! Accessing your dashboards saved you 30 minutes or so, right there. Time is money, so tick, tick, tick your way to all the timesavers that technology affords you. Productivity will soar, and you'll save energy and frustration as well as time (and gas, unless you drive an electric car, and if you do, good for you!).

## Business Software Review Center

Be sure to set aside a weekly session to check out all the new business apps coming onto the market. If you hear a commercial online or see an outdoor billboard about a new business app, make a note. Then check out one of the great review sites to raise your level of understanding about this rapidly expanding business toolset.

## Simple Action Steps to Take Now

- Write down all the apps you have on your phone and laptop. Also add any vendor websites you utilize in the course of a workday, like banks, suppliers, or business media websites. Then start assigning each of these apps to the following categories that best designate them. Figure 8 identifies the specific categories that most of the industry adhere to:

## FIGURE 8

| | | |
|---|---|---|
| UNCATEGORIZED | ACCOUNTING & FINANCE | AUTOMOTIVE SOFTWARE |
| COLLABORATION | COMMUNICATIONS | EMAIL |
| INFORMATION TECHNOLOGY | LEGAL & OPERATIONS | MARKETING & ADVERTISING |

SOURCE: www.squarestack.com

Call a handful of your business app vendors and ask them for a full demonstration of all the tools they offer. Ask what tools are the most powerful and effective, and what alerts and analytics are best to customize for a business like yours.

Pick a category that you haven't deployed a business app in yet that has strategic interest for you. Go to one of the review sites and check out the listings. Pick one or two vendors and arrange demos of their solutions. Have them tell you why you need such a business app.

# COMMITMENT TO TECHNOLOGY ENABLES STRATEGY AND GROWTH

In the first three chapters, you learned the definition of what business apps are and how they can be combined to form your unique AppStack. You also saw how others have deployed their AppStacks and why they need these tools to help them better manage their businesses.

Let's now explore and summarize the huge value derived by deploying the AppStack to its fullest potential and greatest advantage. There are a myriad of benefits residing in all your business apps, and it only takes commitment to extract their value and rationalize the significant investment you've made in them.

## Ease of Use and Time in Hand: The User Experience Calculated

Earlier I pointed out that all business apps today are expressly tailored for the business executive. The app-makers' development teams spend countless hours iterating on their user interfaces as they gather and assess untold hours of feedback from their test users. It's quite fascinating to see just how these UX specialists go about their work.

In fact, it's worth talking about this for a moment. UX is focused on things like the user's feelings, reactions, and perceptions throughout the entire process. In this case, it's focused on designing, building, branding, and launching the app and the ease of use of it.

With business apps, the focus is on the visual. It's all about the navigation, the utility of every link, button, and dropdown menu, and the content and images that support the experience. No pixel is left unturned. You can be certain an engineer has reviewed and reviewed again every space of the experience.

You'll come to appreciate that all these new business apps have not been created or activated commercially without some substantive research and user engagement by the business app-maker. If you really wanted to do some homework on companies that are creating these state-of-the-art business apps, you'll find most of them are funded by venture capitalists. No big surprise, but you'll also discover that most were founded by very smart entrepreneurs who are mostly are engineers, and who take their work very, very seriously.

You'll undoubtedly experience many pop-up notifications or alerts in your inbox asking how the user experience is going. Don't feel intruded upon. Most all of this user engagement has an express purpose in refining the experience. It's mostly done to gather valuable feedback, so be sure to dole out yours. In fact, if you're not being asked for insights on your experience, you should probably be worried about the lack of outreach. By the way, if you've absolutely had enough of the asking, you can refer to your account settings and turn off those messages. But as you engage similarly with your own customers, remember that getting feedback is essential to success.

# Design-driven companies report 50% more loyal customers 41% higher market share

Source: Design Management Institute

The long-accepted adage in our business is, *if you can't generate user engagement, and sustain the regular use of the app, then your app will fail.* For many app makers, they've been able to build their businesses as they've been funded by venture capital. SaaS would not be where it is today if it weren't for Silicon Valley's millions. It's been a critical piece of the innovation in the field, fueling innovation and expansion for the new tools I need. And while this trend has mostly been positive, there are some downsides as well. I'll share some insights into how you can assess new tech tools by looking at how some app companies got started, and the investment strategies that drove their growth.

I previously mentioned that our own company, SquareStack, is an SaaS platform for small businesses. I, too, am very committed to user experience focus and research. I'll share more in Chapter 11.

The lesson is that iterative user interface commitment is about making sure your customers are engaged in a solid, if not spectacular, user experience—from where to click and where it takes them, to the colorful display of metrics and the access to filters and reports.

# Business Apps Deliver Real-Time Feedback

Insights will drive strategic discipline and action. This is about a proactive versus a reactive approach to business growth. What comes with any business app solution is the ability to review real-time metrics, and to call up at a moment's notice the critical data that courses through the specific silo or function that app is engaged for. As an example, let's say you fire up QuickBooks. You may want to know what your receivables and payables look like on a particular Friday afternoon, just as you look at your bank account to see how much cash you have on hand, and you want to check your line of credit before you write a vendor check on Monday morning. Or you may be meeting your freelance marketing executive and need to check the reason for your increase in followers on Twitter, and why they increase at a certain time of day.

You're a business owner. You run an enterprise with a lot of moving parts and the cloud now permits you to jump right in and get a current view of your business at every level. What you're doing is no different than what a Fortune 500 CEO is doing: calling on your departments to report on the current state of things. The magic of an AppStack, as opposed to a half dozen human managers, is that you get reports in real time with the click of your mouse or a tap of your fingers. The time savings alone gives you space to do new things like learn more about your business in a searchable, analyzed manner.

For some time now, Fortune 500 CEOs have utilized executive dashboards to monitor their business enterprises. An executive dashboard is a valuable reporting tool that provides a visual display of organizational key performance indicators (KPIs), metrics, and data. These dashboards give CEOs at-a-glance visibility into business performance across all units and projects.

Figure 9 is a sample CEO master dashboard. Besides all important sales and revenue quantitative metrics, the CEO is provides departmental status reports. Every departmental head of this company, working via their business apps suite, is collecting data and providing a number of filters to analyze the data in a myriad of ways.

And just like you, the mid-sized to large company CEO has neither the time nor the desire to dive too deep into the entire enterprise's data reports. What they want is a "global" view of the company's most important business metrics. They'll defer to the middle managers and line workers to conduct the necessary deeper analyses.

## FIGURE 9

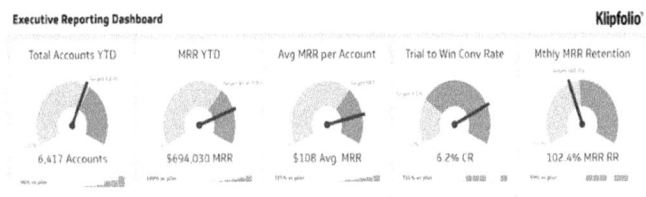

**Executive Reporting Dashboard** — **Klipfolio**

| Total Accounts YTD | MRR YTD | Avg MRR per Account | Trial to Win Conv Rate | Mthly MRR Retention |
| --- | --- | --- | --- | --- |
| 6,417 Accounts | $694,030 MRR | $108 Avg MRR | 6.2% CR | 102.4% MRR RR |

SOURCE: www.klipfolio.com, October 2018

Executive team dashboards are essential tools used by mid-market to Fortune 500-sized companies. Now small business owners can use and leverage dashboards and the insights they offer. I call this "business intelligence in real time." It's time to know every detail of your business, and the master dashboard will be your monitor on all sorts of trends and insights of the enterprise.

Most small business owners are *reacting* versus proactively *leaning into* their resident business intelligence. With an operating AppStack and the dashboards provided by each app, you can extract trends, insights on your marketing, accounting, operations, and more.

In my own growing business, there are many times when I finished our monthly sessions with our accountant focusing on our short-term, necessary payment decisions, and then—*whoosh!*—I was moving on to the next tactical task. I didn't stop for even a moment of strategic brainstorming or to optimize my next decision. With our AppStack and dashboards at hand, I have a combination of short-term tactics and long-term strategies that helps me create more success.

## *Small businesses less than 100 employees have highest rate of business intel adoption, 2018*

Source: Dresner Advisory Service's Wisdom of Crowds 2018

By embracing the cloud and moving more of your technology needs and traditional messy, time-consuming work into our AppStack, you'll recover the valuable time necessary for the strategic side of your business. It's essential that you don't lose sight of strategy: using this technology allows you to become more strategic versus less tactical and reactive.

But business apps alone won't do it. You need a newfound discipline and commitment to looking at your business from a global perspective. Then you need to act on the insights you realize. We'll talk  more about this in Chapter 06, when we look at all the different departments enabled by business apps. Each business app's real-time insights will keep you in a *strategic comfort zone* and help you become a better tactician and delegator.

## App Vendors as Business Partners

As a boomer business guy, I admit that in the first half of my career, technology was not my friend. But then again, it's only been since the 1980s that I've used a computer, the 1990s since I've used the web, and the 2000s since I've used the cloud.

Boomers who've embraced technology have been called *digital immigrants*, while Gen X, millennials, and zillennials are all *digital natives*. However, all of us are new to using the cloud. The story is the same for all of us, too. The cloud and the birth of business apps have allowed all of us to jump into this most critical revolution in how we work at the same time.

No matter your generation, or your level of expertise, don't let technology intimidate you. Hopefully all I've shared so far is impacting your thinking in a positive, creative way. No matter your level of tech savvy, business apps are created with you in mind. Don't forget that you're already a master of your smartphone and the consumer-centric apps you frequently use. It's not a big leap to gain confidence and commitment to the apps that drive your business.

Business app companies with their direct to business selling model have avoided working with the old school tech shops and value-added reseller (VAR) market. Since before the turn of the century, if your small business was growing, you had to consult with these types of organizations. Fees were high, but their expertise was valuable, if not scarce. It was simply a deal you had to do. Don't get me wrong: once you get big enough, you'll need a vendor firm like this and, quite frankly, a CIO/CTO or IT director inside your organization. But most small business owners don't have that luxury.

Research from our good friends at LSA.org confirm that small business owners are still not big enough to support full time technology executives, and certainly looking directly to the app companies for help. Additionally, the existing network of vendors continues to be great resources and recommenders for new technology services. Figure 10 summarizes where small business owners go to buy their business apps.

# FIGURE 10

## WHERE SMB's PURCHASED A CLOUD SERVICE

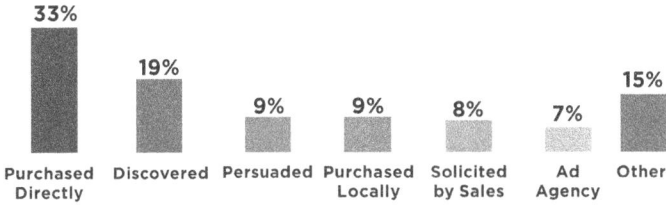

SOURCE: LSA Tech Adoption Index Survey, Wave III, October 2018

It's not just the size and complexity of your organization that leads to discussions on hiring a technology heavyweight. It's issues like these:

- Your processes and technology aren't fully accomplishing what you need, consider engaging a CIO, providing you're willing to empower that individual with the authority he/she needs to accomplish the goals you have set forth.
- Your tech systems just aren't working well together.
- Team members are jockeying for IT resources and you can't continue to referee.
- Departments are battling for control of the tech budget and resources.
- Your technology initiatives are bogged down.

It bears repeating that most businesses under 50 employees don't have a resident, strategy-centric CTO/CIO. Not that it would be bad to have one, but with the rapid innovation, accessibility, and affordability of business apps to form your own AppStack, things just got a lot easier for small businesses.

## It's Not All Roses: Challenges in Building Your AppStack

In May 2018, AT&T surveyed a group of small business owners and discovered the following interesting facts:

- While 75% of small businesses are eager to embrace new technology, 30% find it hard to adopt.
- Over 34% would like to learn more about how to use this new technology.

In the survey, AT&T specifically asked some small business owners what was holding them back from making a bigger leap into the cloud. What they found is that first, it's difficult for many to adapt to the cloud without a budget that can support it.

*"Most small business owners run on a shoestring budget. I do not have extra funds[ing] to experiment," said Alice Kao, co-owner of Alice's Smokehouse. "Unless the solution is proven and cost effective, small business owners like me will steer away from it."*

Another issue with business owners is the dependency they may face with single-source technology vendors. Most small business owners want their risk spread across multiple vendors for a variety of reasons.

*"I don't want to be overly dependent on a system if there's a chance it could ever go away or become a financial liability," said Nick Haschka, CEO at The Wright Gardner.*

*"For example, it would be very harmful to our business if Google decided to increase the price on their G-Suite product line ten times what it is now." Haschka added, "This also creates a single point of failure. When you're dependent on a system, even minor issues can negatively impact your entire business."* [6]

But the irony is that most business apps are from a variety of vendors, thus the issue is interoperability. Can all these apps work in tandem or do they need to? I will tackle this issue later in the book. For now it's good to know that each route to technology adoption and commitment has its tradeoffs.

Last, one constant lament I hear is, "I'm overwhelmed by the choices." [6]

Rebecca West, owner of small interior design company, Seriously Happy Homes, shared that small business owners aren't always aware of new tech. "The sheer range of innovative products and services in the market is extremely intimidating for small businesses that aren't familiar with the tech space," she said. [6]

*Where SMBs would purchase new app services:*
*27% internet service provider*
*15% cloud service partner*
*13% business bank*

Source: LSA.org Tech Adoption Index Wave III

As the business apps market continues to explode, there are new resources filling the gap for the small business owner to learn. I've recommended to many some very useful business software review sites, such as G2 Crowd, Get App, and Capterra to determine which business apps are most applicable to your or your business needs. In fact, in Figure 11 from G2 Crowd's own Small Business Crowd Views you can get a strong sense of the existing commitment to business apps both in terms of growing the Appstack and maintaining investments across the enterprise.

## FIGURE 11

**Core IT Systems in place, deploying, or being replaced by grow and maintain business objectives**

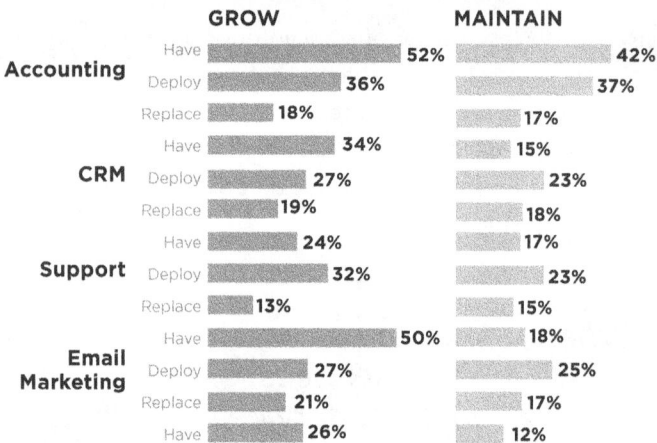

| | | GROW | MAINTAIN |
|---|---|---|---|
| **Accounting** | Have | 52% | 42% |
| | Deploy | 36% | 37% |
| | Replace | 18% | 17% |
| **CRM** | Have | 34% | 15% |
| | Deploy | 27% | 23% |
| | Replace | 19% | 18% |
| **Support** | Have | 24% | 17% |
| | Deploy | 32% | 23% |
| | Replace | 13% | 15% |
| **Email Marketing** | Have | 50% | 18% |
| | Deploy | 27% | 25% |
| | Replace | 21% | 17% |
| | Have | 26% | 12% |

G2 Crowd - Crowd Views/Small Business 2018

Whether you want to add more apps to the stack or replace ones you're not quite satisfied with, these sites are very informative. Reviews are featured from all sorts of small business owners, as well as by their professional review staffs. Also, if you decide to subscribe to SquareStack, there's an app marketplace arranged by category that will guide you through the many available choices.

As I wrap up this chapter, I hope you have a solid perspective as to how technology fits into your overall business strategy and infrastructure. Building your AppStack is essential. You should understand how critical user experience, real-time metrics, and embracing your vendor network are. You should have a sense of what you need to know and the commitment you need to make to fully embrace the cloud.

As a small business owner you're very important to our national and global economies. We're a collective powerhouse and the drivers of much of our expanding macro economy. It's critical that you understand a bit about our collective (and individual) economic power, and as such, why we need to invest at our own business level in technology. If any of the early signals hold true, it's through technology that as small business owners we will continue to lead economic growth, employ and hire more workers, and compete successfully with mid-market and agile Fortune 500 companies.

## Simple Action Steps to Take Now

- Pick one of your existing business apps. Either on your own or with the assistance of the vendor's customer service team, request a full capabilities presentation or "refresh" review. Ask for specific detail on the analytics available in the app, and how to be sure you're utilizing them properly and to their fullest capacity.

- Visit your bank and request a review of all the online tools that can be deployed for a small business. They may send you online, so make sure you follow up. Be sure they present all the best practices and recommendations for their business customers.

Take one of your mundane, old-fashioned tasks (for example, Excel-based customer or project lists, faxing or emailing orders to suppliers, Excel expense reports), and explore the business apps that will *appify* that business task. Sign up for the free trial and give it a proper run.

# THE SMALL BUSINESS
## ECOSYSTEM

So where do you fit into the larger economy? Let's start with the baseline: there are 40 million small businesses in the US that have under 100 employees. The sweet spot is five to 15 employees, where there's an addressable market of about 12 million businesses. Our researcher friends at Facebook have said there are 400 million small businesses globally. Numerous highly regarded research studies are referenced in the exhibit section. One such well-regarded researcher is our own government's Census Bureau. Figure 12 summarizes the power of our community:

## FIGURE 12

| 99.9% | 99.7% | 99.7% |
|---|---|---|
| of all firms | of firms with paid employees | of exporting firms |
| 33.6% | 48.0% | 41.2% |
| of known export value | of private sector employees | of private-sector payroll |

Source: G2 Crowd Small Business Crowd Views 2018

By the way, now is as good a time as ever to share a term that most researchers and marketers utilize to categorize our community: SMB, or small to medium business. Surprisingly, many of our peers don't know this term, and why should they? Besides calling ourselves entrepreneurs, we're likely to declare ourselves by our craft primarily, right? You're a lawyer or a carpenter, not an SMB. For a general definition, here's how most will characterize SMBs: an SMB with 100 or fewer employees is generally considered small, while one with 100 to 999 employees is considered medium-sized.

And some other interesting tidbits about us:

- 51% of small business owners <u>are</u> 50 to 88 years old, 33% are 35 to 49, and 16% are 35 years old and under.
- 69% of US entrepreneurs <u>start</u> their businesses at home.
- According to the National Association of Small Business's 2015 Economic Report, the majority of small businesses surveyed <u>are</u> S-corporations (42%), followed by LLCs (23%).
- While around 9% of all American businesses <u>close</u> each year, only 8% are opened.
- 51% of people asked, "*What's the best way to learn more about entrepreneurship?*" responded with "Start a company." [7]

While these facts may be impressive, I'll go one step further and say that most "every worker is a small business." It's clear now that everyone must manage their careers independent of the company they work for. Statistics reveal that an employee will work at an average of 12 companies in their lifetime. Millennials and the soon-to-join-the-workforce zillennials, are looking at their careers with the aim of eventually owning their own businesses. They see life as a balance of work and play and, thus, view themselves as long-term contractors as opposed to employees of a single employer. The idea that you own your own small business is spreading and becoming commonplace.

Reid Hoffman, CEO and founder of LinkedIn, came out with a book called *The Start-Up of You: Adapt to the Future, Invest in Yourself, and Transform Your Career*. This book is all about how you have to manage your own career and treat your own business skill-sets as a business. That's why you've seen so many join what is now called the gig economy. I'll share some statistics later in this book on how shared services—Uber, Lyft, Airbnb, VRBO, and so on—are examples of the new economy's business models. Many of these new models have encouraged people to start second businesses, or to make that their first business.

When you think about the marketing that dominates the web, television and even outdoor/out-of-home media, you'll find that a staggeringly high number of these messages are being directed toward you as a businessperson or business owner. From personal productivity to advertisements from QuickBooks or AMEX Open, the marketing is all about managing yourself and your business.

*Age of small business owners:*
*33% 50–59 years old*
*17% 60–69 years old*
*4% over 70 years old*

Source: Guidant Financial/Lending Club 2018 State of Small Business

Certainly, you've seen ads from companies like ZipRecruiter and Gogo Inflight. These are companies targeting you as a small business owner or as an independent contractor. Again, you're seeing an incredible amount of capital in the form of advertising being targeted to us, the small business owners.

It's also important to understand that marketers want to reach internal groups within corporations. Many companies have what they call "intrapreneurial" ventures. These are small groups that connect very nimbly in an agile manner. They have separate budgets that are sort of untethered from the corporate mother ship, and are out managing and moving at the faster speeds necessary for innovation. Anytime you hear the term "innovation" it's extremely likely that just under its hood is an independent, smaller group of executives who have been charged by the corporation to spearhead innovative product launches and market introductions. Thus, they're independent businesses, managing their own P&O. The leaders of those nimble, smaller organizations are certainly acting in the manner of a traditional small business.

This reality should prompt such questions as:

- "Do you know someone who has some type of initiative that they're deploying through their regular work environment that's of an entrepreneurial nature?"
- "Do you know people who have side businesses?"

I also think it comes down to our aging population asking themselves, "What more can I do with my life?" Statistics show that many boomers just don't have the savings they need for a safe retirement, so many are launching entrepreneurial ventures of their own.

The baby boomer generation, now in their 50s, 60s, and 70s, who are leaving their corporate jobs—whether voluntarily or through the unfortunate trend of ageism— still need to work. I've heard many stories of them leaving the corporate world without a decent 401K or other liquid assets, and then starting some type of business. Most of them are following their dreams. Whether it's opening up a B&B, becoming a craftsperson, or a financial executive starting his own boutique financial advisor company, they're finding small businesses to launch. With the vast number of new technological tools at hand and the ability to work remotely, it's a heck of a lot easier to start a business today than it was even 10 years ago.

There are many of us who have started shell companies, too, while whiling away at our day jobs. It only takes an idea and $50 to create an LLC online today. Many aspiring entrepreneurs are doing just that, and often more than a handful of companies. While that is only one small step, the trend confirms that more small businesses will be created.

Recently, my wife and I met with our financial advisor. He conducted a detailed review of our portfolio and various insurance plans. Current actuarial tables inform insurance planners to plan out to an average age of 85. This gives new meaning to what (and when) retiring actually means.

In the technology industry, I often see hard working executives who have enjoyed financial success continue to work, but not necessarily in the pressure-packed 24/7 startup environment. They "soft-retire" and serve as advisors, consultants and board members. Not only do they want to stay active, but they're essentially becoming a small business owner. Others on the backend of their corporate careers are looking to more avocational careers after 60. What all of this means is that a majority of boomers won't retire in the formal sense. They're starting their own small businesses instead. The term "retire" is almost becoming irrelevant. Thanks in no small part to the development of business apps, starting a business is much easier and certainly less expensive than it ever has been before.

## *25% over 50 years old Uber drivers*
Source: Uber Newsroom

Case in point: my first company raised $25 million. A good chunk of that was needed to build our technology infrastructure. I could start the very same business today with only mid-six figures in capital. This proves that many of us at every generational level are able to follow our dreams of starting our own businesses because now we can afford to. If we make a mistake, it's less likely that our entire life savings are at risk.

## Technology Reduces Big-Company Advantage

Big companies—mid-sized to Fortune 50 companies— were always able to dominate market segments because of their size. This was in large part due to the fact that they had access to giant infrastructure technology in addition to physical manufacturing plants. Their size is what gave them access to capital expenditure.

The cloud as we know it today simply wasn't available. Smaller companies, unfortunately, had to invest a disproportionate amount of their budgets in technology. This is probably one reason why mid-to late-age boomers have a cynical view of technology—though this is slowly changing. Millennials, on the other hand, who have grown up with technology and known it all their lives, adopt it right away.

Technology is a game-changer for the small business owner. It doesn't mean that they're getting ready to take on Amazon, and have access to as many different products. There's still that challenge. But certainly from a technology perspective, a small business owner can replicate anything that a larger corporation can. As you're going to see through the magic of building your AppStacks and leveraging business apps, you can now orchestrate a complete integrated technology platform. This might consist of your financials, HR, advertising, social media, supply chain deliveries or any combination of these and more — with very little effort all on your own.

## Open Source Isn't Just for Techies

This is a critical message. By "open source" I mean that many tools are being created for anybody and everybody to use. They're being collectively or cloud sourced to come up with a well-accepted, smoothly working software solution for that particular marketplace.

Today small business owners may not be the actual participants in the building of a technology tool within a vertical market, but all the developers in the marketplace are working together. Everyone has probably heard of

Linux. Everybody's certainly heard of Wikipedia. Those are just a couple of examples of open source environments where collective knowledge and insights of a marketplace have created a solution.

## *60+*
## *Number of Zoho community forums*

Source: https://help.zoho.com/portal/community

Most of the business apps that you are or will be using were created out of an open source solution. Many companies have been developed in what is called an open source environment. They are using the collective crowdsourcing ability of a development community to create their unique service. Simultaneously, the smart appmaker creates what is called a user community, or the more familiar term, a "beta platform." Most developers will open up a small community for participants to test the service. The beta users will collectively suggest, corroborate, and review all aspects of the business app service. What may seem obvious is really the foundational philosophy of any committed appmaker.

Many of the tools that we are using have undergone hundreds if not thousands of hours of development where the business app-maker has asked its ultimate buyers to actually help them build the software.

I've already talked about how technology is less expensive and faster. The other important thing to remember here—and this is why I say these technological advances are not just for techies—is that with every business app you use, you can feel pretty confident that your peers helped create it. Every one of the user interfaces that you jump into on in a piece of software, you can pretty much bet that someone just like you—whether you're a salon owner or a car dealer—had another car dealer, a dozen, or more, testing the software before you actually bought it.

The user interface is built for lay people, the generalist small business owner. These business apps are honed and perfected to create a tool that is intuitive, easy to use and, again, built specifically for someone in your shoes. When I talk about our fathers' technology, or technology back at the turn of the 21st century, basically only IT executives and developers really knew how to turn it on, use the filters, create reports, write code, dive in and analyze the data. Today's business app experience is just the opposite. It's built for the layperson. Thus, the techies have made it as simple as possible for anyone with any skill level to use.

## The Gig Economy

As I mentioned earlier in this chapter, today's economy is often referred to as the gig economy. This is about the trend of companies to hire both part-time or temporary workers who work on a project and on an as-needed basis. In the gig economy, the classic small business is the one-person business. According to a 2017 report from employee staffing firm Kelly, there are approximately 50 million free agents in the USA, a full one-third of our domestic economy. Outsourcing site Upwork says that nearly half (46%) of zillennial workers (born after 1997) are freelancers. While this is a classically defined small business, you can bet it is a major trend not going away. And you can bet they are fully engaged with business apps to do their work.

I've met many millennials who are active participants in the gig economy. They drive Uber at night and work as graphic designers while by day. Or maybe they DJ at clubs after working their 9-to-5, bread-and-butter job. Technically, these young people have three LLCs while essentially, remaining a one-person business. You may have heard them referred to as solopreneurs.

I recently met with our accountant, who told me that she has many clients now who submit for a dozen or more LLCs. This idea of having these independent businesses under one umbrella is the trend.

While we were expecting the birth of our twins, my wife and I created a diaper bag for dads called the Baby Bandolier. I spun up an LLC. I partnered with a woman who specialized in designing baby equipment, including strollers and beds. To this day, the product is still in baby boutiques and various online retailers, although my wife and I don't spend a lot of time on it anymore. This makes us part of the gig economy.

Another gigster is a gentleman I recently met who fancies himself a coffee connoisseur. He and his son created a website where customers can buy all the latest, greatest European coffee espresso machines. This gentleman and his son act as the middlemen. They've curated a variety of cool coffee machines from around the world, and make them available for sale in one online place. They've optimized and have their rankings on Google. They take their margin while still working full-time as lawyers. This is yet another example of the absolute and remarkable access an individual can have to starting a business.

I've learned a lot from working toward venture-capital funded companies. One of the early inspirations for me to start writing this book was when I joined the founding team of advertising technology startup, Bizo. There were four or five of us working on a business loan, and we needed to build the infrastructure of our company. We did our research and found all these software solutions. They weren't called business apps at the time, but that's essentially what they were. The team cobbled together our accounting, advertising, HR, and legal apps into what today you could call our AppStack, even though we didn't know that's what it would eventually be called.

The lesson I learned there is actually quite common as an early part of building a business. In my role as a mentor to some of Chicago's leading innovators, the first question that's usually asked after, "How do I raise money?" is "How do I actually operationalize my company?" The magic of business apps is that you can create your company's app infrastructure fairly quickly. Depending on what part of your infrastructure you're starting with, some installations can take minutes, such as a travel app, or an expense tool. Others like QuickBooks may take just a few minutes to open an account, but a good number of hours to actually integrate all the financial data.

With all of the apps available to entrepreneurs and small business owners today, you have all the tools you need to be as creative as you can possibly be. Especially with apps being able to deliver the tools for you to be as creative as you can possibly be. If you're not as creative as you'd like, you can always meet other people and collaborate with them.

Many of these business app companies have online communities that have formed to help users learn how to best optimize the apps. For example, Intuit provides financial webinars. Most app-makers come up from an area of expertise, whether it's HR, operations, financial, marketing, and so on. They often spent their careers in a specific marketplace, and then took their subject domain expertise and invented a better way to get work done. Then they educated their marketplace how to use their apps better.

## Simple Action Steps to Take Now

- Head out of the office early one afternoon and find a quiet place. Spend a few hours mapping out who you see as your competitors. Do this both in terms of traditional (for example, another local similar supplier like your firm) and nontraditional (for example, some web-based company, or perhaps another product category that competes for the same customer dollar). Be sure to write out the advantages and disadvantages they have. Then take a break and review this with your team. Identify what new direction can be planned for a competitive advantage.

- Take one of those very direct competitors, a company possibly you aspire to be like, or find very successful. Go directly to their websites, social media, and take note of what, if any, apps they have enabled for their customer base. I'll bet that they're enjoying success for some of these technology commitments.

- Whatever industry you're in, conduct a Google search

on "apps for your industry." For example, if you're a dry cleaner owner, Google "apps for dry cleaners." Or if you're an appraiser, try "apps for appraisers." Select one of the companies listed and set up a demo of the business app. Ask for a proposal. Take the leap on testing the app.

- Formally or informally, ask some of your best customers to meet with you to discuss their user experience. Five to ten meetings should suffice. Look for their feedback on their digital and in-store experiences. If you want to be more formal in this research you can always create a survey and send it out via email and yes, try using a business app like SurveyMonkey to do it!

# SAAS AND ALL THAT STUFF

You may have noticed that for a book about technology, I haven't exactly taken you under the hood, talked code and algorithms. You didn't think I'd let you off the hook so easily, did you? The following chapter is about as technical as I will get. It's essential that you know something more than the inherent value of business apps and how to build one. So let's now head into what is the most technology-focused part of this book. Bear with me—it'll be worth your time.

I've tried to make this stuff as user-friendly as possible. I've even asked some of my business owner colleagues to vet this chapter for accuracy and clarity of content. However, it still will require your focus and a bit more time to go through it. So my suggestion is to save this chapter for when you have a quiet hour or two to read with minimal interruption. The terms and the various general software applications I'll summarize are at the foundation of the cloud revolution. If you're completely unfamiliar with this or just have a smidgeon of an understanding about it, that's okay. It's time to step up and learn more, so bear with me.

In the previous chapters, I presented terms like the cloud, business apps, and AppStack. At the center of all these innovative tools is the type of software upon which they run. Most of the business apps you utilize are part of a larger category called software as a service (SaaS, or SAS). SaaS is a software model that allows customers to access it online. This service is usually a subscription model and does not require users to install it, but only to sign up for it.

You should know by now that the cloud refers to, at its most generic level, the technology revolution. However, most experts agree that a more accurate definition for the cloud is *the location where (your) data is stored on remote servers accessed from the internet.* It's maintained, operated, and managed by a cloud storage service provider on a storage server (the hardware) that then connects to that very same internet (at higher and higher speeds) to and from your electronic devices.

But that's just half the solution. The other half is the software itself. SaaS is a natural evolution of software. For many years, the old model of using physical disks and installing them on local servers was the only realistic solution. In fact, this client-server model is still required for many scenarios. For larger companies, the technology model required the integrated combination of hardware and software on location to power the company's infrastructure. Often called legacy systems, these arrangements were installed by professional services organizations and maintained by internal teams and the vendors. Don't get me wrong: these systems are still widespread, and often small businesses still rely on them. But many large and small organizations are moving at different speeds to add apps and eliminate on premise (or "on prem") hardware commitments.

## 33% within 6 months
## 33% within 6 to 12 months
## Timing of planned move to cloud tech
Source: LSA.org Tech Adoption Index Wave III

SaaS is becoming the ubiquitous platform for all work in our society. First, the cloud allows for speed and bandwidth that's accessible and affordable to any size company. All of these advances have made it much easier for vendors to enable their solutions and manage their own infrastructure. On the other side of that coin, this allows you to connect efficiently to those vendors, thus permitting them to scale their own technology enterprise economically.

SaaS is deployed in all business areas, such as CRM, document management, financial, HR, ecommerce, management, content management, and collaboration. There are literally thousands of SaaS vendors, but some of the better-known apps include QuickBooks Google G Suite, Zoho, Slack, and Salesforce.

The elements of what makes good software so valuable are likely obvious to you. As I've mentioned, any time you invest money in your business, you had better see some comparable ROI. With software it's no different.

Intuit shared some recent research with us on just what motivates small business owners to buy software and realize satisfaction. Here are the top attributes that others have looked for in a business app:

- 40% Helps them stay organized by better managing the back office
- 33% Helps them maintain good relationships with customers
- 31% Works seamlessly with other software solutions they're using
- 31% Tailor-made for their type of business
- 24% Helps generate sales leads and win new business
- 14% Provides deep insights into their business performance [8]

These should also be elements you look for when you purchase an app. For you to become a better decision maker, not only for the purchase of the right software, but what actual outcome you desire, then it's worth knowing more about this landscape.

The speed and scaling up of the cloud ecosystem, as well as the constant feeding of innovative software for all sorts of end users, has completely and overwhelmingly changed the technology game. It has democratized the power of technology where once upon a time those were tools that only the richest corporations could afford and activate. Now a solo entrepreneur can leverage massive intelligence via the cloud and its accompanying SaaS enabled business apps. No kidding? No kidding.

The digitization of business across every industry is well underway. From ecommerce to procurement, from health to MRO, the ubiquity of the cloud isn't always immediately visible to the naked eye. Much of it is really "under the hood" in many ways. In Figure 13, well-known tech industry researcher Gartner forecasts the continual fantastic growth for SaaS.

## FIGURE 13

**Cloud Application Services (SaaS) in billions**:

2017: **$60.2**
2018: **$73.6**
2019: **$87.2**
2020: **$101.9**
2021: **$117.1**

Source: https://www.gartner.com/newsroom, April 12, 2018

The impact here cannot be overestimated. All patterns of work will be disrupted, and any business owner not paying attention will find it tough going. That is, unless you have one of those businesses where you're not connected to the digital ecosystem. Okay, maybe I will take that back: it's foreseeable that even the charter sailing company or the massage therapist will need to connect via the cloud, too

The cloud has also given birth to more serious, comprehensive services. Mid-market and F500 firms are assessing, too, how they embrace the cloud. Many companies see its value, but have much more complicated needs ranging from security to interoperability of their systems. Many, too, have significant investments in hardware, and need to be judicious on how they divest from one platform to another.

This complexity has given rise to what I call other "as a" services.

## Platform as a Service

Platform as a Service (PaaS) is a category of cloud computing services that provides a platform that permits customers to create, deploy and manage applications without having to build or host the infrastructure typically associated with developing and launching a business app.

Now for a bit of trivia: Marc Benioff, the founder and CEO of Salesforce, is credited as the creator of the term "platform as a service." And speaking of a PaaS business, Salesforce's own App Exchange is a perfect example of this service, as it allows core Salesforce customers to build their own applications on the company's architecture, or in the Salesforce cloud.

## Infrastructure as a Service

Infrastructure as a Service (IaaS) is a service model that delivers technology tools on an outsourced basis to support a company's internal operations. IaaS is an integrated complete solution that provides hardware, storage, servers, and data storage.

## Business Process as a Service

Business process as a service (BPaaS) is a term for a specific kind of web-delivered or cloud hosting service that benefits an enterprise by assisting with business objectives. In the general sense, a business process is simply a task that must be completed to benefit business operations. Using the term (BPaaS) implies that the business process is being automated through a remote delivery model.

The term BPaaS folds into several ideas based on earlier types of web-delivered or cloud hosted services. One of the earliest was software as a service (SaaS). In providing SaaS, vendors found they could let clients access software over the internet. The old model entailed selling it in boxes in conventional retail stores and charging licensing fees for setup. This kind of menu option software purchasing became popular with businesses, and vendors started to improve on what they could offer.

Now vendors offer all sorts of services delivered through cloud technologies and the global IP network. Just a few of those services include items like PaaS, IaaS, and IT as a service (ITaaS). Business process as a service often involves putting several of these options together to completely automate a business process.

For a concrete example of BPaaS, think about certain kinds of tasks that businesses may need done on a regular basis. One example is transaction management. Credit card transactions may need to be recorded in a central database, or otherwise handled or evaluated. A vendor that can offer a company the same task performed and delivered through cloud-hosted networks would be an example of BPaaS.

*+309% increase in cash flow*
*due to cloud tech adoption*

Source: Microsoft Survey with Thought Arbitrage Research Institute 2018

IaaS, PaaS, and BPaaS are all primarily services focused on mid-market to Fortune 500 companies, most would agree. However, for companies in high-growth mode with more complex needs, it's never too early to explore these "scaling up" solutions. Any of your current business app providers and vendors can provide advice on how your organization can assess whether this is an option for you. If it is, they can then discern what partners they work with can accelerate your technology aspirations.

Cloud technology overall (and more specifically these "as a" services) are allowing businesses to analyze all sorts of data and adapt their business models quicker than the competition. Being a cloud-powered small business is a clear competitive edge, and will thrust you ahead of most other companies. It allows you to compete against bigger companies, and to focus on your core business offerings without having to invest significant resources or time to scale the technology infrastructure.

Small businesses are recognizing the value of public cloud solutions as they accelerate their digital transformation. The need for agile, low-cost solutions will continue to increase along with security and performance capabilities. With the changing landscape of the business apps ecosystem, future cloud tools will be more secure, reliable, and vertical-specific to facilitate profitable and durable small business owners. Quite frankly, if you don't make the move to the cloud and build your AppStack, you may be running a slowly dying, irrelevant business. While some businesses may continue to soldier on without the need of current technology practices, most will definitely be impacted by not joining the necessary revolution.

The cloud is already well entrenched in our digital workflow. Apart from possibly a few outdoor-based business models, face-to-face physical engagement businesses, and craft-based enterprises in non-machine environments, you're likely touching the digital work ecosystem. Here are just a few ways that others engage the cloud:

- The retail clerk calling up orders on the CRM system
- The lawyer working with government websites to check client's probate status
- The contractor measuring a floor with their software connected tool
- The event planner sending out evites to their client's database
- The jewelry maker posting new work on Instagram
- The shipping agent managing their drivers via a tracking software
- The salon owner sending out their Groupon promotion to the local community

Think about what software, vendor portal, or information site you engaged with today on your smartphone, laptop, or desktop. How many different "hats" did you wear today? And with that hat on, what type of software did you dive into? How many types? Two? Three? Seven? Most of your activities are now enabled via business apps.

## *53% small businesses adopted CRM*

Source: LSA.org Tech Adoption Index Wave II

Next, let's take a round-robin of the most popular SaaS solutions as well as leading brands within some of the primary categories.

## Payroll

Payroll SaaS is likely a cornerstone of most progressive small businesses, if not your own. As you now know the inherent benefits of SaaS, payroll is a natural category of software that can make paying the bills and your employees much easier.

SaaS payroll is the DIY of payment processing that any SMB with little accounting background can activate and manage. It's especially attractive for the SMB that has headcount constraints and business owners who must run payroll themselves. Several easy steps via a typically well-designed intuitive user Interface let you:

- Access your accounts by logging onto the service provider's secure website
- Enter your payroll data and relevant pay rates and tax info
- Approve and process payroll on a regular or automated cycle

The platform handles the rest. Most services will provide an employee portal for their own management and information, which allows the owner to save substantive billing coordinator and payroll employee costs. Compared to the legacy services, whether it's big companies like ADP or your local accountant at $75 hour, SaaS has shown its competitive advantage as it's now the dominant solution for SMB owners.

Leaders in this space include Surepayroll, another Chicago-based company. I know one of the founders there, Troy Henikoff, who saw the financial challenge inherent in running a small business. He and his co- founders built a great software solution for the SMB, likely out of his garage or apartment. Surepayroll attacked a market challenge, raised capital, and eventually sold to a competitor called Paychex. Surepayroll is now part of a burgeoning category of business apps.

Other companies you may have heard of include Paycor, ADP, Gusto, Zenefits and Intuit. As you can probably imagine, the category is getting crowded. Financial tech (fintech) is now a term. It's one of the most funded categories in business technology, as smart financial entrepreneurs see many opportunities to disrupt old school lending, funding, wealth management, and traditional banking with, yes, SaaS. Venture speculators are more than happy to write checks, big ones at that.

I'll cover the financial apps category in more detail later, but as it goes in all functional categories, where there's a crowd of innovators, there are also a few likely failures. Some of the most likely reasons they failed are that their value proposition did not hold, they ran out of cash, or just didn't execute well. Buyer beware.

## SFA/CRM

You've probably seen the acronyms SFA (sales force automation) and CRM (customer relationship management). We techies sure do love our abbreviations. Outside of association executives, I'd bet we rank a strong second in coming up with shorthand names for our solutions.

Sales force automation (SFA) and CRM, right alongside Financial SaaS, are probably the most embedded systems, especially with companies who place huge value in their customer database and its attached data and insights. While SFA is still used often, it really applies to a subset of CRM. Since most small businesses don't have large sales teams, it's less about managing those execs' databases and accountability, and more about directly working on the customer and prospect pools.

The SMB clearly has direct relationships with their customers, whether in-store on the phone, or face-to-face at home. All those relationships—their histories, purchasing data, engagement with the company—all directly feed the customer database. CRM is the essential lifeline to the revenue.

## Google G Suite: AdWords, AdSense and Analytics

Google is such a familiar brand, as are its group of services, that I forget that these tools are foundational to many small businesses. Google has an absolute dominant presence as a default email system. Its digital advertising tools—especially its self-service platform, AdWords, the number one outbound advertising service for driving sales—are crucial to many small business owners' success in reaching and attracting new customers.

And for those of you who consider yourselves publishers, Google AdSense is also a key revenue creator. Many small publishers have told me that the gravy train of AdSense revenue is long gone, but that it still provides a decent incremental revenue stream with no real costs attached.

Google Analytics is another service many small businesses utilize to track their website performance. Not only does it reveal how many visitors click on a site, it also tracks their time spent there, as well as providing key audience demographics and insights into a customer's intent and behavior. As mentioned frequently, the small business owner needs to review these valuable metrics, extract their value, and apply the new knowledge to his/her business, if it's to be of any lasting value.

As Google is very good at launching ancillary services, so you can expect more cool tools in their SMB Suite, including, among their newest offerings:

- Video and voice conferencing
- Secure team messaging
- Shared calendars
- Templates for documents, spreadsheets, and presentations
- Low-code app development environment
- Cloud storage options
- A universal search tool across your entire set of Google solutions

Because these tools all integrate beautifully, they allow a business owner to kick off its AppStack with just one supplier. However, while it's more cost effective and provides a simpler activation process than most, you should know that all your data will be stored on the Google cloud. Be sure to very carefully read the privacy and data policies of Google G Suite. Additionally, there are many parts of your operation—marketing, HR, financial, and such—that you should pay attention to regarding their privacy procedures. App-makers comply with industry best standards. If they didn't, they wouldn't get funded nor get decent market penetration. It's always worth checking out to secure that extra sense of confidence when it comes to your data and your customers' data. I will be talking about SMB data and privacy later.

## Intuit/QuickBooks

This is another anchor piece of software for most businesses. Intuit/QuickBooks remains innovative as they continue to add features and new partners within their service. With nearly 6 million customers, they're the industry leader in more ways than one. To date, our company SquareStack still uses QuickBooks Online and I have no complaints.

However, compared with some of its competitors, QuickBooks is not inexpensive. By checking online reviews at G2, Capterra or Get App, or even SquareStack's own review section, you'll see the many new innovative SaaS players now in the market.

Intuit, the corporate parent, is adding scale to its wide offerings, and here are just some of the tools with which you can augment the basic QuickBooks service:

- Mint
- TurboTax
- Intuit Payroll
- Intuit App Center

I find the last service of special interest. Intuit App Center is emblematic of the proliferation of business apps. Intuit sees an opportunity—a big one at that—to provide its existing users a curated library of financially specific business apps. There's a lot to be said for working with just one vendor for a set of solutions. In the Intuit App Center, you'll see apps like:

- Tax1099
- American Express
- Amazon Business
- Apptivo Invoices
- Bento for Business
- Billify
- Expensify

See the trend? All of these apps are mostly geared to the financial services arena. It's not surprising, as it fits their corporate positioning. Similarly, you'll find in the recruiting business apps category companies like ZipRecruiter, that integrates all the job board apps, and Salesforce, which aggregates all sorts of plug-in business apps in the realm of marketing and customer engagement.

And so far, only one company—news flash! self-promotion alert!— SquareStack aggregates all functions of the enterprise in one consolidated approach for the small business owner. We can't rest on our laurels, however, because there will be more challenges coming.

## Facebook

Do you have your Facebook page open now? Did you see our ad for *Appify Your Business?* Just kidding. But it's not outside the realm of possibility. Seriously, Facebook is another foundational platform for many small businesses, primarily for those serving a consumer audience. But I will say, even those small businesses selling to other businesses see value in having a Facebook presence.

For many small businesses, Facebook is often only a default and online homepage, or a strong partner to the company's brand website. All good marketers see the value in building a dialogue with their customers, and if you promote your Facebook page in all of your marketing, then you'll have an audience to talk to. The worst thing you can do is *not* talk to them.

I strongly recommend that you post every day, or at least a few times a week, as the impact can be amazing. If you can't do it yourself, assign your son, daughter, or one of your millennial workers to do it for you, or have them teach you how. You simply cannot afford not to know how to do it. The information you share on Facebook is up to you. However, I recommend you use your page to provide news on sales, fun stories about the company, share positive experiences of your customers, or show off your civic and community engagement. The Facebook page is an "always on" customer relationship medium, and the best part? It doesn't cost anything.

What can cost, though, is the Facebook advertising system. For those who have used Google AdWords, this may be worth a look. With Facebook advertising, you can filter your ideal market audience through geographic, demographic and other signal targeting. And like Google

Ad services, you can track that prospect's activity all the way to the point of sale, or at least start a dialogue with them going forward.

## Twitter

Ah, Twitter, such a controversial platform that always seems to be on fire with dissension and division. I will leave the political and fake news discussions for others, but I will say, Twitter is an obvious communications platform that, if used correctly, can be a critical channel to reach your prospects and customers.

You need a handle, and you need to tweet. It does no good to open an account and not tweet. It takes a conscious commitment to do so, but just like I suggested with Facebook, delegate the daily postings to a staff millennial or make sure you do it. And like all of your social media, keep your messaging confined to promoting your business, sales, community engagement, and company news. Don't make it a personal platform unless there's an issue you feel very strongly about, either as the owner or as the employer of many families. This is just my opinion, but I believe you're far better off if you limit the sharing of your own opinions to your personal social account.

One key tool in many social business apps is the ability to post to all of your accounts. On Instagram, for instance, you can simultaneously send the same post to all of your social media platforms. There are social media management apps like Hootsuite and Sprout Social that can do the same, as well as measure all the inbound engagement by followers and customers.

## LinkedIn

LinkedIn features many tools that any small business owner can leverage. I should know, as the last company I worked for, Bizo, was acquired by LinkedIn, before I started on this journey. For all small businesses, LinkedIn is a solid recruitment platform for several vertical industries. No doubt their strength lies in how they engage with both recruiters and workers looking for new employment opportunities, especially for those in the mid-market to Fortune 500 segment. But it's also a great tool for the larger or small businesses, or especially B2B firms.

While LinkedIn claims to be a community of business executives, and they continue to push content and network alerts to members, like Facebook for Business, if you will, most small businesses still haven't discovered its many features serving small business. Most small businesses are not "joiners" as they don't have the time, and from this position they assume too soon that there's no value in the platform.

If you're a small business selling to other businesses, LinkedIn has solid marketing options. For example, you can use their advertising system to reach very specific market segments. Let's say you're a lawyer for environmental IP. You can also go on LinkedIn and target companies in the energy, landscaping, construction, and waste management segments only. Who knows? This is a solid approach to help fill your business development funnel.

Build your brand on your business's LinkedIn page by showcasing your expertise, product, and services. Content marketing on LinkedIn can balance your investments between organic and paid efforts. While you advertise, you can also post, just like you do on Twitter and Facebook. Be sure to have your employees join in, too. Also be on the lookout for content from your suppliers that you can deploy on all your social pages.

Last, in the course of business development, be sure to sign up for LinkedIn's InMail feature. I've used it for all our business development efforts, and it can help you gain access to high level decision-makers who are typically difficult to reach.

Something to watch out for here: Microsoft bought LinkedIn several years ago, and I have yet to hear of any "synergy" product announcements. As you have seen, many of the bigger app-makers for small businesses have built broader toolkits, and I imagine that the Microsoft Suite will soon be integrated with LinkedIn. Imagine being able to plumb for sales leads via Sales Navigator, and then onboard those profiles into Microsoft CRM. Or porting over messaging from your company PowerPoints into your LinkedIn posts. Talk about high-powered potential for exponential growth!

## Financial Services and Credit Card Companies

Certainly, financial vendors are central to all our businesses. What's amazing to me is the progress that these companies have made in developing digital engagement tools. Tools that let you conduct your banking and financial work without having to leave your home or offices. You don't even have to physically visit the bank to deposit a check in many instances. Mobile banking is for real, and the changes coming will further digitize these important relationships.

This is yet another category that really screams self-service, doesn't it? We all know the hell of being put on hold, or dialing through a voice-operated menu to get to the right automated message. There's so much ground to cover here, and I can't get to all of it, but I will share some top-line ideas for you to consider as you look at your array of financial business apps.

If you want to save time, automate as much as you can from the service suite your bank and credit card vendors offer. Also, work with your accountant and be sure they're involved in helping you integrate all you can in your financial functions area. It really is worth the few hours to review the toolkits and turn them on. A few of them that I've activated at SquareStack include auto bill pay, mobile deposits, cash on hand alerts, paperless reporting and line of credit integration.

The options are also numerous with your credit card vendors. Again, work with your accountant and be sure you're integrated where you need to be. Take advantage of adding on services and online activation tools. We're living in an era where self-service will be the primary way to bank, and brick and mortar financial institutions may well become obsolete. Look at what has happened to the majority of newspapers and magazines since the advent of the digital age rising, if you doubt this possibility.

## Business Services Companies

While we all run to FedEx, Staples, Office Depot, or OfficeMax for another box of pens, paper, or a print job here and there, you can bet they see the light of the appification of business. They also recognize the disruption of companies like Vistaprint, Stamps.com, moo.com, and Uline. All these companies are great disrupters by basing their models online and providing customers in-app purchasing.

Of late, you're seeing these legacy physical stores push innovation by building business apps and directing prospects and customers to their apps and website stores. Office Depot and OfficeMax's latest apps let you do a lot. They provide 24/7 customer service and free delivery of projects that cost $35+ both in-store and online. They also allow free in-store pickup. Like most smart brick and mortars, they're leveraging their physical assets along with the big budgets behind their online initiatives. And in November 2018, they announced that they'll open office space sharing and compete with the likes of WeWork.

There's an interesting company in Chicago called Fellowes, a manufacturer and distributor of office equipment. Their equipment line includes shredders, air purifiers, binders, and computer accessories. Fellowes has built a substantial network of suppliers and dealers in retail and B2B. To support this network, they have built an app that can be branded with the dealer partner's name and logo. They're basically powering the business appification of hundreds of retail organizations. Search for "Fellowes Mobile App" on YouTube.

Many will take this path of helping their customers appify their businesses. At SquareStack, for example, I work with our channel partners to brand and sell direct to their captive vertical audiences.

*2.6 million*
*Number of apps in the Google Store*
*2.2 million*
*Number of apps in Apple App Store*
*600,000*
*Number of apps in the Amazon App Store*

SOURCE: Statista December 2018

## Amazon

Some of you are likely shuddering right now at the mere mention of this online behemoth. Others are incredibly thankful for the services Amazon provides you and/or your business. A whole book could be written—and probably more than one has been—on how Amazon has disrupted pretty much every business on earth. But in this book, I just want to share some high-level insights that will confirm your own views, or be a big wake-up call for you. It could be said that "Amazon is eating the world."

Let's first start with AWS, their somewhat quiet, yet gigantic B2B business. AWS—otherwise known as Amazon Web Services—is their cloud-hosting enterprise and is likely one of the top profitable divisions in the Amazon family. In February 2018, Amazon shared this news: AWS grew so quickly in the past decade that it's now the fifth-largest business software provider in the world.

Revenue at Amazon Web Services jumped 43% in 2017 to $17.5 billion, representing about one-tenth of Amazon's total revenue, the company reported. The only publicly traded business software companies ahead of AWS are Microsoft, IBM, Oracle, and SAP, according to data from FactSet in April 2018.

AWS revenue growth accelerated in the second quarter, rising 49% year over year.[6] Holy cloud (pun intended), now *that* is big business! It's gotten where it has by providing companies highly secure, scalable services, and without signing a long-term contract. They're especially adept at providing a host of other tools as well. This is yet another confirmation that the bigger companies are building their app exchanges to connect with their core platforms.

Their partner network has all sorts of complimentary services, all at good pricing. These provide technology business applications in areas such as disaster recovery, analytics, AI, big data, mobile and game development. SquareStack has been a long time AWS customer, from our first beta site to our now substantive network of channel partners. What you should also know is that AWS can customize their services, so if you're not a technology trained exec, you shouldn't feel impeded.

Now onto the Amazon shopping platform: the system that has changed so many businesses, large and small. For a number of small businesses, Amazon's web store is the most important platform upon which small businesses sell their wares. In a press release from the company dated January 2018, small businesses currently account for half of the products sold worldwide on Amazon. More than 140,000 small businesses' selling surpassed $100,000 in annual sales during 2017, according to the ecommerce giant.

Amazon further detailed that more than 300,000 US-based small businesses joined Amazon Marketplace in 2017. Amazon Lending, another part of Amazon's B2B service sector, surpassed $3 billion lent to small businesses on Amazon since it began in 2011. Most of this is for the SMB retailer, and should be leveraged along with all your other distribution channels.

In September 2018, Amazon introduced a new shopping destination within its site called Amazon Storefronts. It showcases SMB products exclusively. It contains a "curated collection of over one million products, and deals from nearly 20,000 US small- and medium-sized businesses." The site also promotes small businesses with videos and profiles (stories). There are over 25 product categories. Well worth investigating.

As for how they're building further focus on the likely expanding business segment, according to a recent survey conducted by one of our research partners, Local Search Association, roughly 70% of SMB respondents said they're members of Amazon Prime. Of those, 72% are using it to buy parts, products, or services for their businesses. Amazon is disrupting the actual supply chain of SMB procurement, which obviously is being duly noted by aforementioned Office Depot, OfficeMax, and Staples.

While many of the big box retailers and a variety of other "physical" sellers of products have been hurt by Amazon, the smart SMB retailer is outsmarting the big boys by recognizing that Amazon is a great friend. To summarize then, Amazon is a highly cost-effective vendor for both technology services and anything you need for your workplace. It's also a scalable and trackable storefront that reaches the entire world. I will be talking more about Amazon and strategies to drive your SMB success later in this book.

Lastly, you should be aware that you need to optimize your product listings and copy with search optimization in mind. There are web vendors now that can help you raise your profile for all those shoppers searching in your product or service categories. One more thing to think about, and if you sell through this channel, it's essential you invest in Amazon search engine optimization.

## Apple iTunes and Google Store

These app marketplaces are now the gateway for any consumer facing service that is depends on their App for their primary customer gateway. Getting your app into this marketplace is essential to scaling your business.

Submitting an app to iTunes isn't as simple as clicking a button, but it won't be that complicated either. It's really a submission process open to app makers and just requires filling out an application on site. Here are some helpful sites that will summarize the process for you:
www.instabug.com/blog
www.codewithchris.com
Or go direct to Apple's developer site at https://developer.apple.com/app-store/submissions/

For Google Store and Android apps, similar resources are available:

www.hiddenbrains.com and search for "getting an app in Google Store"

www.turbofuture.com and search "How To Upload & Publish Android Apps For Free"

Or go direct to the Google developer site: https://developer.android.com/distribute/

Remember if you are selling to consumers, you need to be in both stores.

For B2B businesses, it does no harm to be in these stores but it will be more critical to deploy other distribution channels to get app adoption. Those include social media, business software review sites, and industry business media sites.

## BYOB Apps

BYOB? Does this mean what I think it means? No, not beer in this case, but *bring your own business* app. Yes, the time has arrived that any SMB can have their own app. It's less expensive or daunting than you may think. Many companies are going down this path to serve their customer base and are even getting exposure in both the Google and iTunes stores.

There are several companies that can help you build your own branded app, including Buildfire, Zoho, Appypie, and Altova. You can even go to freelance project board Upwork and find an inexpensive developer. What is key to remember here is that as your audience becomes more mobile-centric, especially around shopping and research, the greater you must be in committing to build out your own app strategy and resulting tool. It's going to be table stakes in the next 12 to 24 months.

Congratulations! You have made it through the most technical of our chapters. You'll be dangerously smart at your next social event. But seriously, if you have captured any insights here, I hope there's cursory knowledge, or a confirmation, that you knew more that you thought, and that you see the absolute need to *appify* your business.

## Simple Action Steps to Take Now

- Ask all your vendors whether they are indeed SaaS-based solutions, and if not, whether they're considering moving to this platform. Ask a few of them to explain more about the benefits and features inherent in an SaaS-based solution.

- Set aside some time in the next couple of days to learn more about SaaS. You may wish to start by going to these company websites and spend a few hours reading about this trend and how it is changing everything about work:

  Technopedia
  G2 Crowd
  Capterra
  Udemy

Udemy is an especially intriguing website, as it's all about online education. This particular course will inform not only on the principles of SaaS, but also offers insight on whether your small business should actually build its own business app!

- Investigate your local market's "app developers," web development firms that specialize in building business apps for small business owners. Once you decide on a few of them, ask them to demo their work. Then request their insight on how a business app would work in your line of business. Be sure to find out as much as you can around process, pricing, data, and time required. Maybe this can be a next quarter strategic commitment.

# THE STATE AND MIND OF BUSINESS: THE INS AND OUTS OF STRATEGY AND TACTICS

As Sun Tzu once stated, "Strategy without tactics is the slowest route to victory. Tactics without strategy is the noise before defeat."

Starting with strategy, how often do you find yourself just plain tired, like you're on some endless loop of mental cycling, or stuck on a treadmill? How much time do you think you spend putting out fires versus spending productive planning time? Sound familiar? If so, it's safe to say you're overwhelmed by the tactical. No shame in it, but it's the most common and detrimental pitfall for an entrepreneur. To make a course correction, you need to commit to strategic time.

To this point, I've discussed the revolution of cloud technology, defining what it does, and helping you begin building your own AppStacks. Additionally, I've shared insights with regard to buying and using business apps to make your businesses more efficient, economically vital and durable.

I've also talked about the size of the marketplace. The small business market itself is one of the largest in the world. As such, the small business owner has become an even more important part of today's economy given their passion, focus and willingness to embrace cloud technology.

## Technology as a Driver of Strategy

Now let's talk about how technology will catapult you into being a strategy expert with the time to put those great ideas into action. More time will organically emerge as the result of the efficiencies of these new technologies. Every small business owner and startup alike are so entrenched in day-to-day activities that they're mostly just reacting to one-off issues and challenges they face in every given workday. As such, because each and every day is replete with the same necessary urgency around putting out fires and multi-tasking across the enterprise, the investment in strategy is severely limited. I would venture to say it's nonexistent for many.

That will change with embracing a technology platform. Doing so will provide you with a whole slew of insights and data, right at your fingertips. Not to mention that managing internal activities will be much more efficient. This means that you'll now have more time to look at your data in a very deliberate way: what's working, and what's not working. You'll be able to discern what's trending well and what's not in your business so that you can make better-informed and more deliberate strategic decisions.

*25% of UK-based SMBs*
*don't have a business plan*
Source: Talk Business UK 2018

How are you doing with combining strategy and execution? There are countless great books written in the area. I'll leave it to the many experts to provide more comprehensive insights. Below, is my personal go-to formula. It's comprised of four stages that I find balance the fine mix of strategic output with tactical execution that follows a strong vision. Getting even just some of this right will scale your success. And by being committed to your AppStack and the real-time insights they produce, you'll have a very effective feedback machine. Here are the steps:

## Build Your Strategy

- Turn your vision into a clear pragmatic statement. Keep it real in terms of achievable goals.
- As your strategies take shape, ask for honest feedback from customers, employees and vendors. Do you have a sense of your company's value proposition? Do you need to improve the proposition?
- Are you sitting around just waiting for change to happen, simply following your industry's routine business model?

## Translate Your Strategy into Your Daily Routine

- Are you passionately following through with tactics that will drive the strategy? Everyday you and your team needs to allocate energy to the new strategy. Communicate it so that everyone understands the critical mission at hand.
- Are you supporting the strategy with investment in infrastructure, and training to build these new services?

## Execute the Strategy

- Are you motivating your team to support the new strategy? New incentives, and the ability to provide feedback will ensure buy-in.
- Are you keeping track of the team's performance? Your business apps in HR and internal collaboration will permit detailed performance measurement here.

Strategy is the initiation point that leads to the deployment of tactics to support that strategy. I've found that many small business plans lack a clear strategy for growth. If a company has received financial support from angel investors—venture capital or the like—you'd better believe a substantive business plan has been written that becomes the lynchpin to building that business. That business plan is what tipped the scales, convincing the investors to become involved. But many small business owners, whether they're salon owners or car dealers, don't have any kind of written business plan, period. This fundamental lack creates extra urgency to be more strategic about your own game plan as you build your business.

The scope of this book does not include information as to how to write a strategy statement. There are already many books available on that very topic, and I urge you to seek them out. I strongly encourage everyone to become more strategic about their business. Strategies within a small business can range from the kind of retail distribution you would like to have in the next 24 months to the number of customers you would like to bring aboard in certain categories. It could be how you plan to redesign the physical venue of your business. All of these are strategies. Tactics are what you use to execute these strategies.

If you want to redesign or expand your internal office space, one tactic might be to hire a consultant to review and assess your present office space. Another tactic would be to have your real estate agent provide you with some details as to how these architectural consultants have designed other offices for their clients.

*30–50 pages*
*Recommended length of small business plan*
*1 page*
*Length of AirBnB's early stage business plan*
SOURCE: Talk Business UK 2018

Again, a strategy will inform your tactics. But what I find in the day-to-day life of a small business owner goes something like this: The day is spent in a tactical frenetic environment where small business owners are always reacting, as opposed to being proactive. What this means is that by the end of a difficult workday, you're completely tapped out on tactics as opposed to focusing on what's most important, which is your business strategy.

## The Importance of Collaboration

I once worked with a startup in the ad tech industry that had built a platform for marketers to automate their advertising buying. Their CEO had a very broad-stroke, high-concept business plan with which he raised $250,000. I was one of the advisors to his team and met with him every month.

This CEO's business plan failed because it lacked strategy. Specifically, his plan focused solely on tactical activities-whether it was to secure a technology vendor, for example, or pitch certain pilot customers. He failed to share a strategic plan with his team of six to eight executives—all of whom were part-time or contract employees—so they were working without a clear definition of their end game.

Typically, at any company I have run or partnered with, I recalibrate our strategy plans every quarter. They don't change all that much, quite frankly, but this process of recalibration certainly gives the team an opportunity to engage, discuss and and strategize so that we are all on the same page and can adjust our tactics to reach those goals. Most of the strategy statements that I've seen startups and small businesses use consist of a very concrete set of goals built around customers and aspirational KPIs within the organization, upon which their tactics are matched.

KPIs are a measurable value that demonstrate how a company is achieving key business objectives. Most companies use these to evaluate their success in reaching those targets. Even at a small company level, it's not out of the ordinary to have a set of goals defined this way. For a salon owner, these might include adding a new chair to their existing four, or booking 50 hair appointments per chair each week. I'm certainly not the expert in this vertical, but certainly these types of goals are great ways to incentivize and build your business.

*7 Top KPIs for small business*
*Cash flow forecast*
*Gross profit margin as a percentage of sales*
*Funnel drop-off rate*
*Revenue growth rate*
*Inventory turnover*
*Accounts payable turnover*
*Relative market share*
SOURCE: Intuit/Quickbooks

One of the hardest things about strategy for small business owners is that often, these seem like lofty, less substantive dreams. These are not as tangible as the day-to-day seemingly mundane activities that comprise the running of their business, like issuing payroll, meeting a customer, or reviewing an employee's performance. All of these are most definitely very concrete, tactical and necessary endeavors. When you spend a half-hour or 45 minutes looking at what your strategy can be, it doesn't come with the same kind of internal payoff that a small business owner is used to.

Small business owners are motivated to start their own businesses for a variety of different reasons. As technology continues to provide deeper access to all the metrics of your business, it's absolutely essential that you understand and utilize these new technologies to help you become more strategic about your business. Something as easily committable as 15 minutes a day spent assessing the real-time metrics of your business will not only help you become more strategic, but ultimately more successful.

At SquareStack, over the last 18 months, I've observed an inflection point where many small business owners understand the value strategy. This is when they embrace CRM.

Many small business owners have committed to this technology, this business app, as part of their AppStack. Often, it comes wrapped in other technologies that they've bought via other suppliers, like QuickBooks or Zoho.

When a small business owner commits to becoming a CRM practitioner, all of a sudden, I believe that owner moves into a new understanding of their customers. With that ongoing knowledge now at their fingertips, and their commitment to understanding and marketing to their customer, CRM in a sense, releases them to become more strategic in the way that they go about their business.

Because time so defines and can limit a small business owner, one thing you need to get clear right of the bat is that strategy isn't something that happens in an afternoon. Strategy is a long-term business objective, be it over three months, six months, one year, or five years. Thus, the idea of committing to such an expanse of time is more than a little bit challenging for the small business owner.

For example, I have a list of 22 to-dos today, and none of them have anything to do with strategy. But this Friday, I'm meeting with two of my partners and we're going to spend two hours talking about our strategy and goals. I find that the more you formally schedule strategic discussions, whether on your own, or with your partners or lead managers, that collaborative time is still worth your time investment. Remember, tactics are only effective when they match your strategy. If you don't have a clearly defined strategy, all the time you spend on your tactics is wasted.

## Simple Action Steps to Take Now

Review your to-do list for the day/week. How many items are strategic, forward leaning versus reactive and tactical? I will bet the majority are the latter. Take a hard look at the list and substitute or add some strategic-centric activities. Just a few quiet hours a week can do wonders to your future planning, self-confidence and the health of your business

- If you have a team of staff members, contractors, or both, arrange for a team brainstorming session for a few hours. Tell them to come to the meeting with their thoughts on how the business can "digitize" to modernize itself over the next six to 12 months. Gather and summarize the outcomes of the meeting in writing. From that document, commit to some strategic initiative that the team buys into.

- Have you actually written out a one-, two-, or five-year business plan? If you have, when was the last time you revised or refreshed it? If longer than a year, it's time to update, hone and sharpen it. This doesn't have to be an enormous undertaking, in fact, you can choose to make it fun! After all, it should be driven by your vision, dreams and realities of building your small business. Formalize this dream into an execution plan.

This will do wonders for you and team, especially when things go sideways.

If you need some resources, do a Google search on "business planning software." Or visit G2 Crowd, Capterra and Get App company websites.

# THE HIGH C'S:CRITICAL DIGITAL STRATEGIES TO EMBRACE AND EXECUTE

Let's take a break now from the technology deep-dive and move on to what I call the High C's of SMB technology adoption. You may recall from college marketing 101 classes the 4P's of marketing: price, product, promotion, and place. Or perhaps you learned other mnemonics from a Young Presidents Organization (YPO), or any leadership seminar, such as the five C's of leadership: competence, courage, confidence, communications, and coaching skills.

Now it's our turn. I think you'll find the High C's included here worth the read and reference, as you commit yourself to your business technology plan. It's a list to which I've given serious thought, and it expands to include some fundamental business strategies. So these are not just technology goals in and of themselves.

## Customer > Everything Starts Here

Probably no argument here, as nothing happens without customers and nothing grows without happy customers. If you aren't focused completely on your customer, you shouldn't be in small business. I wanted to start with this tenet, even if it sounds so completely self evident, as you'd

118

be surprised how many owners really don't embrace this Golden Rule. You need to have a personal relationship with as many customers as possible and be sure your team also follows the Customer first mantra. What follows, you will see how each High C relates directly or indirectly to the customer.

There is always a business app! CRM and Insight tools are plentiful: Gainsight, Totango, Optimove, Client Success, Periscope.

## Collect > Data

Data is ubiquitous. Every digital action produces data, and that data resides within your SaaS platforms. It lives in your bank accounts, your social media, your day's receipts. As a consumer, you're likely concerned—if not downright dismayed—by just how much data companies and organizations collect.

But as a business owner, you must strike a balance with your consumers' concerns and ethics and how you want to go about collecting and leveraging the embedded insights dwelling within that data. Most small business owners I know have only cursory knowledge about their customer data, much less how they collect it. Very few others are conducting proactive assessments of the data's insights.

Make sure you understand the privacy policies that police your current customer-facing business apps. It's imperative that they honor the industry's best practices. Don't be afraid to be assertive in asking to review their policies. Again, most of your software vendors are likely part of an industry association, and are mandated to follow what the industries collectively create in terms of ethical data collection. Just never assume. Find out for a certainty, and stay informed of any policy updates or changes.

In this book, I'm zeroing in on more of the strategic and high-level tactical stuff, so here are just a few pointers:

- Be sure to review and get comfortable with how your vendors collect data.
- Speak in common, layman's terms. Don't speak in technology blabber.
- Be transparent in how you collect data from customers. Give them a clear and visible option to say yay or nay to offers you make. In marketing language, this is called "opt-in." Don't bury the privacy policy behind several asterisks and links. Your customer will appreciate the transparency and authenticity.
- Ensure your customers and yourself that your data is safely guarded. Be sure you completely understand the security systems that protect your data. This goes for customer-facing business apps as well as your internal business apps like QuickBooks or employee-facing software.
- When collecting data on customers, always be sure you're applying best practices. Respect customers' privacy and you'll be on the right side of the ethically committed business community. If you're not sure if you're already adhering to standards, the first place to start is with your vendors. Your software partners are likely well-aligned in their own data policies. They wouldn't have been funded nor enjoyed market success if they were not playing by the rules. If you want to do your own research, go to godaddy.com, or thedma.org for more information on best practices.
- Make sure that the data you collect in every one of

your business apps use the same "taxonomy." For example, you'll want to know Twitter and Facebook handles, general demographic information, and standard name addresses, along with emails and phone numbers in each app so you can unify this data in aggregate. For most SMB Owners, this is a later stage initiative, combining all you know from all your channels into one "Omnichannel" view. But for now, at least have a similar data template in place.

There is always a business app. Most SMB's aren't ready for a CDP (Customer Data Platform) but it's worth taking a look at them: Segment, Exponia, Tealium, Listrak, Full Contact.

## Capitalize > Finance Online

Fintech is exploding, and the SMB market is a key target for these rapidly emerging companies. As I shared in earlier chapters, you should educate yourself on all the online tools your legacy finance vendors offer. Additionally, convert old-school paper to online alerts and communications. There's an inherent cost savings here as well. Banks and financial vendors of all types are incentivizing small businesses to activate online-only relationships. This pattern will only continue.

*Top three tech budget priorities*
*35% productivity*
*35% financial*
*34% security*

SOURCE: Salesforce SMB Business Trends Report 2nd Annual 2018

What is more exciting, though, are the many new funding platforms and business apps that are helping small businesses find cheaper money for scaling their businesses. This also applies to providing key services to streamline their internal financial systems, and thus save time and money.

I've come across companies like FundBox, which I compare to a Rocket Mortgage for SMB Loans. In real time, you can apply and find out what sort of line of credit they will authorize. Bento for Business is an expense management tool that takes the pain out of expense reporting.

Financial apps are at the core of our enterprise. You may want to check out some of the tools that will augment your foundational software such as expense management, loan apps and forecasting. Check out Expensify, Concur, Fundbox, Lending Tree, Zip Forecasting.

## Competition > Who Now?

This may seem obvious, but with an ever-growing digital tool library, you can find some expedient and automated ways to track a raft of competitors. There's an an entire new category of business apps called competitive intelligence. All the review sites I reference in this book have a myriad of solutions worth checking out. Again, any business apps that are priced right and are possibly relevant to tracking your competitors and what they're doing are worth knowing.

At the top of this list of these powerful tools is—guess who? Alexa, owned by Amazon. It offers site audits, keyword research, competitor analysis, and audience analysis as part of its subscription. And if you're an AWS customer or part of their storefront business, well, you can bet you can buy the bundle for a good price.

Crayon can track the web presence of all of your competitors. With most competitive intelligence (CI) business apps, there's a question of how detailed they go with the companies they track. One company that can provide some great aggregate competitive info is Yext. If you're a B2C business, you're likely already allocating some search-marketing dollars, and as such, it would be good to know what the other guy is doing. Yext's new service allows small businesses to track up to five competitors (local or national), showing how your company ranks against your competitors in local search. It can also monitor how your store locations rate against your competitors.

Now step back a moment. While your closest competitors are readily apparent, give some thought to who your new competitors are. For example, if you're a local haberdasher (gosh, I wish there were more of you) now a company like UnTuckIt, the online shirt seller, is a competitor. If you're selling legal services, there are two new competitors: Legal Shield a low-cost online legal advisor, and DocuSign, a repository of all sorts of legal contracts and templates.

If you are a search marketer, try Adgooroo and SEMRush to assess competition. Watch what your competitors do with their websites via Crayon.

## Curricula > Learn and Teach

Always be learning. If you stop learning, you stop living. You never graduate. You have surely heard these words of wisdom. But I can absolutely confirm that most small business owners often don't take this to heart and keep learning. They think they know enough already, or just rationalize that they have no time to learn. Like all things in life, without consistent commitment and discipline, business success can be a pipe dream.

But with content so accessible and so rampant, there's no excuse not to make a more serious commitment to learning. Be sure to consult with your associations, who, if they're doing their jobs well, are curating the relevant content for your continuing education. Subscribe to a few newsletters in your field or function—but not too many so that you become overwhelmed and tempted to ignore them all. Regularly reading those that you find most pertinent will be a nice proactive predictable education track for you.

As mentioned in earlier chapters, lean into your business app vendors as they have plenty of webinars, in-person conferences and newsletters. There is value in many of these, despite an echo of the obvious self-serving purpose to increase their own profitability. A lot of software companies have user group communities, which is another great way to get proficient at their solutions and to meet like-minded peers. One of the more famous and productive small and mid-sized communities is Amex Open. I know many small business owners who find this community invaluable for advice and counsel.

There are also great small business media platforms that cater to our community, some in print and some exclusively online. *Inc.* comes first to mind, along with Ramon Ray's *Smart Hustle*, Smallbusinesstrends.com and

FitsSmallbizness.com

G2 Crowd is another interesting, if not vital, platform where community is becoming foundational to its business model. While they're all about business app reviews, the community is what's driving those reviews. There's really nothing better than peer reviews to help you make a decision. Be sure you check them out.

WIthin each of your resident industries, there will be a leading business media company, and you ought to seek out their resources. In the machine shop industry, for instance, there's a sizeable, well-regarded forum group called Practical Machinist. This community has over 1.1 million monthly visitors and 150,000 registered users. The dialogue and networking engagement takes place among machinists from large companies like Tesla, GM, GE, and AMD, on down to the countless small business owners working in that industry.

In the technology industry, among coders and IT directors, there's another substantive community called Spiceworks. Here thousands of technologists exchange best practices and issue project RDPs.

Name any industry, and some smart publisher or association has created a community to network in. One last one worth sharing here is Dental Town, https://www.dentaltown.com. It was started over 20 years ago by Howard Farran, originally a practicing dentist. He saw an unfulfilled need where dentists wanted to share best practices and learn about new technology. Howard's community now has over 250,000 dentist members. He launched Orthotown and print magazines as well. He has authored a number of books about building a business, too, which are well worth checking out.

Be sure to check in with your industry's associations and business media resources. Do this not only for their expert content, but also for education and networking opportunities. Doing a targeted Google Search is often the simplest and most productive place to start.

There is always a business app. Linked In Learning (formerly Lynda) and Pryor Learning have prodigious content libraries. And as the owner, you need to educate your employees, so be sure to check out  LMS (Learning Management System) apps like Canvass, Blackboard and Google Classroom.

## Content and Curation > Produce, You're an Expert

Never forget that education is a two-way track. Be sure to position yourself as a domain expert to your customers and prospects. Don't underestimate the value you can provide to your customer with timely, relevant content. You have the ability, if not duty, to push curated information to your audience via your social media pages, newsletters and on your website. You're a trusted vendor, and as such you have the preeminent position to build an event that truly engages your buyers and goes a long way to building and/ or strengthening your relationship with them. Consider your customers lifetime buyers. Build that conversation online and in person.

*70% of consumers prefer to learn about
company through articles/blogs than ads*

SOURCE: https://www.demandmetric.com/content/
content-marketing-infographic

I recommend you read any book published by Joe Pulizzi and Robert Rose. They built a business around a discipline called Content Marketing. In fact, you have probably already noted Joe's introduction at the front end of this book. He is the real deal, and I was lucky enough to work with him a few years ago. This is a long-time relationship and yes, reading his books is the core motivator behind why I wrote this very book.

Being fully transparent here, my goal was to gather all the hard-earned knowledge I have about business apps, share it with my fellow small business owners and leverage my "expert position" to help grow my own software business, SquareStack. It's not crazy to think you can do the same with your own business, and seek to scale your success.

This arena is chock full of apps and many are integrated with your marketing systems. Here are some tools worth bolting on to your CRM. Business Content management via Sharepoint, Box or Dropbox. Content Distribution via Taboola, Outbrain or ShareThis.

## "Cost Per" > Know What You Get

As you have learned in your social, search and CRM campaigns, the rubber meets the road when determining your cost per lead, cost per download PDF, cost per customer visit, cost per missed workday, and cost per returned check.

Most of the analytics portion of your AppStack can help you filter down to an individual transaction. Keep this in mind as you get smarter at your business apps. And as you automate these trackable signals, it will inform you on how to invest, divest or recalibrate your capital and resources.

There is always a business app. The Amazon Advertising Suite has a number of tools to analyze your advertising placements. Also a group of apps that help you analyze Social media impact include Sprout Social, Zoho Social, HootSuite and Mention.

## Cloud > Ubiquity in Service

The cloud is here to stay and most of your services are in the cloud or on their way. Remember this as you look at your day-to-day activities and think about how you can become more efficient and economic in their doing. There's probably a cloud-based solution.

Of course, the Cloud is what powers most every business apps but let's talk about the Cloud here as the host platform for your business and its data. Amazon Web Services is a leader in Cloud hosting and we use them at SquareStack. Others include Microsoft Azure, Google Cloud Platform, and Cloud Foundry.

## Commerce > Selling All the Time

If you're selling a physical product, there's no reason why you shouldn't have a commerce-enabled website or at the very least, a product directory with definitive information on how to transact and transact quickly. Many web development services can activate commerce solutions as part of their suite. Thus, adding it on is certainly a simpler integration than it was a few years ago. Pricing has come down dramatically, too.

You're also using your social media to run buyers back to your site's shopping page, or you may use Amazon and their store tech to sell products. If you're a restaurateur or run a service company, you should quickly assess and deploy your offerings on the many digital channels available online. A few examples include car dealers on YouTube, plumbers on Angie's List, and craft-makers on Etsy. Make sure you're leveraging their full toolkits. I bet there are lots of these out there that you have yet to explore.

Those of you who have hired a web developer or work with a firm like SquareSpace, you likely don't need to spec out an ecommerce solution. But it doesn't hurt to know what these business apps can do for your online selling. Check out some of these firms: WooCommerce, Shopify, Big Commerce, and GoCentral.

## Community > Social Now, Share Now

I talked about how you as a small business owner can find ways to network amongst peers. But that directive should also be heeded for your own customers and prospects. At the foundation of social media strategy is the idea of stirring the pot of all your fans, customers and prospects. There are no better advocates for your brand than these. And in the venue of social media, if your followers are providing good feedback, then you have some real magic.

Extend this out to live events like store celebrations, networking events, and local street fairs. This lets people see your brand in a new light and amongst like-minded peers and buyers. In our local community, there's a realtor who not only is a prolific newsletter guy, but also writes a column in the local paper and sponsors a "Dancing in the Streets" event. Mike McCurry of Coldwell Banker is the exemplary progressive SMB Marketer, and he has established a trust in the community that is hard to find in a small business. I joke with him, though, that I'm tired of seeing his mug on all those For Sale signs!

Your community extends to your own website and promotional arsenal. There's no better method than to feature customers' testimonials on why they like your product or service. Encourage your customers to connect. There are a host of web services where you can build a social network right on your site. While I know that's a bigger commitment, I've seen small business owners execute this, and am positive that more will do so as the price decreases, and the ease of activating becomes even simpler.

Lastly, I need to talk about the downside. With opening a community and adhering to transparency, there will, of course, be the naysayers, the bad customer experience or a bad review. It's going to happen, so just expect it. It's pretty much the nature of the beast. Some of these things may already have happened to you or your business. Just bear in mind that in our current world, the one initiating the negativity can just as easily be a sly, unethical competitor at work as an actual disgruntled client or customer.

So when you see these, don't take it personally. Take a breath and objectively assess the commentary. It is more critical to step back and see if there are any common threads in the negative reviews. If there are, then you likely have a bigger issue that needs to be addressed. I believe some review sites, specifically those like Yelp and Airbnb, highlight the actual frequent "descriptor" words mentioned in all your reviews.

Always respond promptly. Don't let a bad comment fester. And answer authentically. Just as you do on the phone or in person at your check-out desk, customer service best practices lead the way to continued success, and they should online as well. A complaint well-handled is as valuable a testimonial as a long-time happy customer.

In addition to social networking apps, you should investigate chat software and review software that could be embedded in your website. Both of these tools encourage conversation and input that is exceptionally valuable for your business. Also, if you don't have SurveyMonkey or similar research software, get it today. Leveraging your captive community to unearth insights and recommendations on how you're doing is a savvy move.

You'll get feedback about your reputation as a vendor, as well as learning what will enhance your customers' experience. If you're wise, immediately take action on the quality suggestions and ideas, and guess what? Before you know it, you're likely to realize repeat and larger sales from your existing customer base.You might even consider holding a contest for Best New Business Idea among your customers, with some type of prize offered to the winner. People love contests!

There is always a business app. There is an opportunity for you to build your own community on your site and within your customer database and here are a few solutions that enable a community platform: Higher Logic, Discourse and Vanilla.

## Customer Relationship Management > Engage for the Long Haul

If statistics bear out, about half of you are committed to some CRM strategy already, or have the software goods but haven't activated the potential of it yet. The other half is not even close. There's no greater leap in your AppStack than the moment you commit to CRM. So many small business owners that have crossed the gauntlet on CRM have told me it was their best decision ever.

This building block of your AppStack is all about insights into your customers and prospects. It's also the unifying nervous system to your entire tech investment and subsequently the success of your business. By activating CRM, you'll have access to your data in real time, and insights will emerge on all sorts of levels. Some of the outcomes will include:

- ROI of your advertising
- Engagement metrics of your customers and prospects and divisible by all sorts of filters
- Ability to target segments with messaging specific to those customers

- Interlinking metrics of inbound and outbound marketing success
- Ability to record all sorts of activities including sales, contracts, and employee engagement
- After a website, social media, and financial software, I'd place CRM in the essential foundation of a quality AppStack.

This is a core technology and many of you likely have a solution in place but there are areas that may warrant further diligence. Pricing, interoperability and industry focus are all criteria you need to regularly assess. Check out these other leaders in CRM: Zoho, Hubspot, Pipedrive and Nimble.

## Collaboration > The Co-optive And Competitive World

Collaboration may seem like an obvious initiative, but let me give this more context. Collaboration means many things in this digital world. I want to emphasize that collaborating can now be done online, and with less than obvious collaborators. First off, most of your business apps partners have 24/7 helplines and chat tools. As the app-makers leverage future users to build and iterate to a valuable user experience, you can bet they want to hear from you often, and at any time of day. It's how all this stuff works and works better.

Also, you'll find in this appified world, new partners will emerge. For instance, you may be selling one primary product, but maybe that product will sell better with an additional complementary product. Get out on the web and track down those relevant suppliers. It's not that hard. Or post in a professional community what you're looking to do in terms of promotion and partnership. Again, it's not too hard to do and you may be surprised at what comes of such an inquiry.

You may also find that your competitors become collaborators. You may find working with a competitor may create some new and mutual opportunities for you both. What is the saying? A rising tide raises all boats? I can vouch for our own business, SquareStack, that I initially feared thought one company, much larger and funded by millions in venture capital, would crush us. Happily, however, now they're one of our best channel partners.

The appification and digitization of the business world requires a focused, if not wary, 360-degree view of your competitive set. Who would have thunk that Harry's would challenge Gillette, or that Casper (the bed maker) would challenge the dominance of retail bed sellers nationwide?

If you were to look at a new solution to your stack, a project management app for your team should be in your consideration set. Lots of stellar performers in this category such as Basecamp, Asana, Hive, and Monday.

## Conscious > Socially Mission Your Enterprise

You may think this is the trendy, liberal leaning thing to do. But you'd be wrong. So many businesses now are building social purpose into their DNA. It's not only gratifying at a personal level, but it motivates employees, partners, and, yes, customers as well. More citizens of the consumer economy want to align their own values with the companies they frequent. It seems obvious, but if you see similar benefits, prices and customer service between two vendors, what if one was a supporter of the local YMCA? That one nugget of giving back may move you to select this vendor.

*Top 3 challenges in adopting new tech*
*53% budget constraints*
*49% not enough usage to justify*
*48% difficulty in customizing tech to business*

SOURCE: Salesforce SMB Business Trends Report 2nd Annual 2018

Also, for those of you starting businesses that are socially or environmentally focused with your actual product or service (such as solar power, redevelopment of poor communities, or electric car chargers), you should investigate applying as a B Corporation. A B Corporation is becoming a legitimate option for these types of businesses. B Corps balance purpose and profit. They're legally required to consider the impact of their decisions on their workers, customers, suppliers, community, and the environment. And the outcome is significant: people want to buy, vendors want to sell, and investors want to underwrite these types of companies. It certifies that a company is serious about the environment and the people connected to their enterprise.

There aren't any social mission apps per se, but there are a few charity based business apps that are worth exploring. This is a way to align technologically your business' broader social philosophy into a platform that can enable a socially motivated practice. Apps in this field include KindLink and Charity Engine. There are volunteer management solutions too, like Causecast and Involvesoft.

## Cynic > Be Wary and Be Objective

I probably don't need to encourage you to be more cynical, do I? But it plays an important role in managing expectations, and level-setting your plans. In our case here, I want to apply cynicism specifically to how you assess and buy technology. As a startup guy in technology, I can admit and firmly vouch that there are a lot of "pretend" software companies out there, as well as firms that really aren't committed to the small business marketplace.

I know that choosing a software platform is an important decision, but what is more painful and time-consuming is *moving off one failed platform to a new one*. So, the key is to make sure you select the right business app right out of the gate. Do your homework in the review sites. Talk to peers, and rigorously demo the candidate solutions. Ask for a test period and customer references. You're smart and likely do this with other vendors in more traditional old school categories, so don't be bashful. So what if you don't know all of the right questions to ask? Just be transparent and inquisitive with the business app company you're considering.

I will refer back to the software advisory and review companies like G2 Crowd, Capterra and Software Advice. They are great resources to stay apace of business app ratings.

## Cyber > Be Safe, Not Sorry

I've talked about this a few times in the book. But since you have joined the business app revolution, even if you have a lonely website, you own a lot of data. It's a core asset of your business, and you must ensure its safety as well as the safety of your bank accounts, and ecommerce system. While the big companies are often attacked by hackers, that does not mean they won't find an SMB site to exploit.

Be sure you have reviewed your AppStack vendors' security systems and follow the best practices they suggest. Also, be sure to adhere to basic things like username and password protocol. Don't use Kanye's password (000000) or your name again. For your customers, leverage double opt-in protocol. Basically, this is the process where the user submits his or her email address in the subscription form on the website and clicks "Join our mailing list." Then the user receives a special confirmation email in which he or she needs to confirm his or her wish to be added to your mailing list. Make sense?

Always use a backup service, like Carbonite, that backs up all your personal and business data. Be sure your website and email vendors have all the current tools activated to protect your website and email. Again, most business app makers are playing to the industry's standards, but don't assume that is the case. The act of asking and walking through their toolkits with them will relieve your anxiety. Not only that, it will also teach you a few more valuable lessons about cyber security.

Security and Privacy will always be critical for the small business owner. It's a good practice to look at additive features to your existing infrastructure. You need to protect your user name and password assets. Check out SquareStack, Okta, and Lastpass. For data protection there are business apps such as Box Zones and Gravity Zone.

I'm finished with the High C's and heading back to port. I hope this shorthand list was worth your time. Keep it close at hand and I'm sure you'll find some new rituals for your tech-enabled workday.

## Simple Action Steps to Take Now

Incorporate three of the High C's into your next quarter strategic goals. For instance:

- Start your own social media page and commit to personally posting once or twice a week. Put in a repeat calendar reminder for a few morning 20-minute slots and honor them.
- Conduct a thorough system audit of all your security features for your website, business app vendors and your own personal social profiles.
- If you don't have your devices connected to a backup service, get it done now!

# 09

# YOUR TECHNOLOGY
# PUNCH LIST

It's essential for you as a small business owner to have a web presence. If you don't, it's time to get one. Past time, really—but not too late—just hurry up and do it right! Not sloppily, mind you. If you're in this category, you'll find there are plenty of experts available for hire to get you online professionally and pretty quickly. Understand that the majority of potential customers will get their information about your company online through your website or social media.

So it's vital that you take a strong interest in building a user-friendly website, and pay attention to your traffic and promotions. Treat your site as though it's your physical storefront.

There are lots of ways to build or improve a website, from companies like SquareSpace, GoDaddy, or your Yellow Page vendor, as well as small web developers in your town.

While a good number of small business owners still don't have a website, they're using Facebook as their default homepage—especially if they're a consumer business. You absolutely must run both Facebook and your website in tandem to ensure that you're getting complete coverage of your local market.

*64% of small businesses have a website
36% do not*
SOURCE: Clutch.co

As millennials become your core market, you have to communicate to their default way of consuming information. That means keeping up with Instagram and Twitter, if not on a daily basis, then certainly a few times a week. Keeping your social media channels updated is just the nature of the beast. If you fall behind or merely maintain a passive presence, you and your business are not going to seem engaged with the market. And you had better believe that your competitors are going to notice Also, make sure you place all your Facebook, website addresses and all of your communications in your marketing collateral, including your business card. It's absolutely essential that you communicate through all of your various channels, completely across all of your platforms. For local business especially, make sure you check out Google Business and claim your spot. It's free and a powerful means of gaining and tracking search engine results.

## Instagram

If you have a business that's based around consumer products that are best viewed in illustrations and photographs, then I suggest you build a strong Instagram presence. Instagram is becoming a very important resource for many consumers as it allows them to actually see what your products look like. It also provides the opportunity to explore different ways they can assess those products while also building their future wish lists.

Compare this to many of the ecommerce sites that you already visit, whether it's Amazon or Zappos, where you can place future purchases in a folder, in a cart or on a wish list. Many consumers are using Instagram as an early-stage research tool for products that are better assessed by looking at them.

If you're a lawyer, repair shop owner, or other business that primarily offers services as opposed to products,Instagram probably would not play a major role for you. But, if you're marketing purses, sports gear, or literally *any* kind of tangible products, Instagram is a great site for marketing.

## e-Newsletter

Another important part of being a good marketer for your small business is the necessity of having your own company e-newsletter that you send regularly send out to your customer and prospect database. No doubt, this database either resides in your CRM system, or in your Constant Contact email platform. Perhaps it's simply sitting in an Excel file. Wherever your database resides, it's essential for you to facilitate and create an e-newsletter where you can feature current offers and discounts, as well as highlighting happy customers' testimonials about how much they love your small business. Your newsletter should also share stories about the company, knowledge or specific resources that the buyer can use to explore the particular product areas you offer.

Naturally, you want to stay in touch, understand your customer better, and keep your brand top-of-mind with your customer base. Therefore it's essential that you include an e-newsletter in your marketing mix. The best thing about a newsletter is, if your customer database opts-in and declares their desire to receive your newsletter, then you have a readymade captive audience. Another benefit is that there are no hard costs in communicating with your database on a monthly or weekly basis—as opposed to buying ads in the Yellow Pages, the local shopper or the city newspaper.

All of these hard copy print options are all but obsolete in today's digital age, so it's vital that your business reaches out online, and possibly through SMS text messaging as well. Make sure your database clients grant you permission to text them. Most professionals would agree that e-newsletters are the most efficient way to market to your customer database, and gone are the days when you need to send newsletters out by snail mail, unless your consumer base demographic contains lots of seniors. In that case, you may wish to consider printing and mailing newsletters by the good old USPS.

As far as opt-in goes, I'm sure you as a consumer have long lamented how you're overwhelmed or angry at all the irrelevant, unsolicited and undesired advertising that you receive on the web. It's of maximum importance to make sure that your database opts-in to receive your newsletter before just sending it. This is all about respecting people's privacy and their online security. Just search "Opt-in privacy policies," on the web. Your web developer or marketing person should be able to access these templates so that as you create your newsletter you're honoring the best practices that both the industry and, soon, our government, will require for you to publish a newsletter and engage with your audience.

You now have to be sure your product is "search optimized" on Amazon's product search

## Hire a Millennial Digital Geek

I've found that many small business owners benefit by hiring a millennial who better understands the digital landscape. Essentially, the rapid leaps the digital age has made in recent decades and millennials were born to be together. Recruit an intern from the local college or high school by posting notice of an internship on any local recruiting site or job board. If you can, seek out web developer classes and any that specialize in social media, and look into talking with the instructors or department heads about making your needs known to the students. You can recruit a digitally adept intern or a paid part-timer who can really do the groundwork for you. Then roll your sleeves up and start social posting.

It comes naturally to most. As a small business owner, you've hired people across many parts of your business. Assuming you're skilled at hiring smart people, here's a good, inexpensive and plugged-in way to drive your social media marketing and other digital tactical work: Hire a young person who is looking to build their resume as they move into the workforce. These are digital natives. You don't have to teach them new software. For them, it's plug and play, as they say. But do watch over their work, making sure your voice remains true to you and your business in everything that is posted.

## Bookmarking and Research

As you get more adept at managing your technology through business applications and building your AppStack, the theory is that you'll have more time during the business day for strategic, proactive activities. One such activity is to take 15 to 30 minutes out of your day to research your market segment, focusing specifically on technology adoption. Depending on your business, you may not need to do this every single day, but certainly should keep your finger on the pulse of this a few times a week. This could be as simple as keeping up with local business media, vertical industry websites and blogs, or doing simple Google searches.

Commit a decent amount of your time to learning about apps. Build yourself a folder where you can house these links if you don't have time to read them all in the moment. I've been doing this for years. I have a folder on my desktop and in my mobile phone where, if I'm reading a certain article, I'll just bookmark it and save it to read later over coffee—or something stronger.

*Most helpful groups in making a purchase
decision
46% other business owners using the product
or service
27% staff/employees
10% vendor*

SOURCE: The Alternative Board (TAB) Oct 2014

It's easy to get caught up in our day-to-day activities. But you need to carve out time to learn to be proactive. It's an investment that will not only keep your business afloat, but keep it forward thinking and up with current trends. This translates to higher profitability, and costs nothing but your time and willingness to learn, so why wouldn't you do it?

## Local Webinars/Seminars

The benefit of the local seminar is that you can also network. Webinars and archived podcasts are great because you have more flexibility in terms of how and when you listen to them. For example, you could even listen while brushing your teeth in the morning and preparing for your day. It's not like you have to carve extra time out to listen, so they're great for multitaskers!You can listen/watch them at your convenience.

Local seminars are also great ways to meet other like-minded entrepreneurs, build a network of connections and resources, as well as vendor possibilities. It may often be difficult for you as a small business owner to take the time to get out and learn. If that's the case, you'll find that many companies that provide online webinars. These can range from your vendors—who often educate their clients—to universities and local chambers of commerce. There may be small business owner Meetup.com groups or something similar in your area. It may prove to be well worth your research efforts to check it out and participate in the ones that feel most productive.

You just need to become better disciplined at spending more time around learning and finding pragmatic solutions to some of your everyday problems and challenges. Build a steady diet of networking within your community. This is vital to stay top of mind with your customer base. This includes networking physically, and/or online via your vendors, your industry media or associations.

Another increasingly popular option are podcasts. There are certainly plenty of podcasts within the technology industry. For instance, LinkedIn has podcasts daily about how to use the site as an advertising platform and more.

Also, if you're a member of an association, they usually offer continuing education programs. These are certainly a rich repository for continued learning. Many annual conferences by the leading associations are doing real-time webcasting of those conferences, so you don't have to incur that $10,000 travel expense to go to Las Vegas, no matter how much you may want to!

## Business App Reviews

Since you're reading this book, I'll venture a guess that you're interested in becoming better informed about your technology and its management. It only makes sense that you continue that commitment by reading business app reviews. I've provided a list of some of those sites. Just like you review travel on TripAdvisor, you can look at various reviews of business apps.

SquareStack has aggregated a variety of reviews into one library. If you're looking at your email and find its current condition clunky, just spend a few minutes on review sites. Look at what other email services make sense for someone who runs a business in your vertical markets, and compare all the benefits, upsides, downsides, and pros and cons of the software.

You're probably using iTunes or Google Store for personal or consumer sports, travel or health apps, so why aren't you doing the same for your business? SquareStack offers some of the well-received review sites for business software and the small business owner.

## Company Reputation and Review Business Apps

If you are a B2C business, retail centric in your customer base, it is essential you monitor your company's reputation. There are a number of solid software offerings that can track how your business is faring amongst your target market, customers and prospects alike.

Restaurants know too well how Yelp can impact their business and contractors the same with Angie's List. Every year there are new online review sites and service aggregators that are creating other distribution channels for your business. This is great in one respect but also means you need to monitor more platforms on how your business is faring.

*Top 4 tips for managing data security*

*1. Automate backups and build in redundancy*
*2. Consider server virtualization*
*3. Run a full-service security suite*
*4. Have a big-picture disaster preparedness plan*

Source: https://www.sba.gov/blogs/4-ways-safeguard-and-protect-your-small-business-data

## Reputation Management and Review Management

Software companies are multiplying to serve this important new discipline that all retail operations must include in their marketing mix. Refer to these categories in the software review sites to assess what tool may be right for you.

## Account-Based Marketing (ABM)

If you are a B2B facing business, you need to pay attention to this rapidly growing marketing trend.
In a nutshell, account based marketing is a strategic approach to b2b marketing based on specific account/company awareness in which your business considers and communicates with individual prospects at certain companies or companies by name. The idea is that by targeting these companies at the top of your funnel, you can build awareness amongst all the decision makers and eventually secure qualified leads. There are many software

and marketing services companies addressing this market need. It's not for everyone, but it is worth exploring

## Simple Action Steps to Take Now

- Assess your current social media commitments. Make sure you're on all the major platforms, and take personal responsibility or delegate it to a team member to post a few times a week on all channels.

- Post a part-time job or internship opportunity online, or contact some local colleges in pursuit of what I call the digital geek. Hiring this young go-getter for just a few hours a week will be a blessing and a big time-saver. Appoint him/her as your default team member for all things digital. Activities could include the above posting (with some training), researching business apps, coding, and onboarding new technologies. And because they're in the loop of the constant influx of new technologies, they just may be able to teach you a few things!

- Commit to attending some local networking events specifically around technology. Consult your local or neighborhood chamber, call Yext or Yellow Pages companies and ask about any events they may have. Also check in with all your business apps vendors, as many are providing educational opportunities, whether in-person events or online webinars. Lastly, check in with your favorite industry specific business media company. See what events they may be putting on around technology. Most are moving in that direction.

- If you are a B2C organization, check out a few of the review sites within your category. Take a deep dive into how your business is being reviewed by customers, share these findings with the team and brainstorm what trends emerge, both good and bad, from the aggregate insights of customers.

# "ALL IN" COMMITMENT TO TECHNOLOGY

Always remember, technology should be your friend. It shouldn't be like some mysterious IT director that you're afraid to meet. It's all about embracing the cloud, which was built specifically for you, the small business owner. As a small business owner myself, I've taken this journey. I was a publisher and sales executive for most of my career. But in the last 15 years, I've come to understand technology and use it to my benefit—as an individual managing both my career and the businesses with which I've been involved.

It's impossible to avoid technology, so get comfortable with it. This is about creating your own digital sphere.

I'll start with what I call mastering self-service. I'm sure you've noted that as a consumer, at many retail establishments you now have the option of self-checkout. This may be at CVS, Walgreens, or even at Costco where you fill your cart and leave without any bagging or customer service assistance. The same is true at every bank, and every credit card company, where it's all about paperless monthly account statements sent to you via the internet whether through emails, texts, or app notifications. Snail mail in these spaces has pretty much gone the way of the dinosaur.

You'll note the self-service mantra being pushed upon you in every segment of your life. You could say that it's because technology makes it easier. But it also simplifies the life of the vendor you're buying from: self-service translates to cutting costs by eliminating several jobs now rendered moot.

You're definitely going to see self-service continue to become a routinized ritual in both consumer and business lives. Word has it that Amazon has opened its first self-service retail store where you literally walk in, grab groceries, drop them in your bag and walk out. All of your purchases are scanned wirelessly. You'll get the bill on your credit card in real-time. But how does this pertain to your tech stack and business apps?

They're all being built with the idea that you can run these applications on your own. The sooner you understand that and embrace the idea that everything is going to be self-serve, you'll find yourself ahead of the game.

As I said earlier in the book, most of these new business apps have been designed with the layperson in mind. I talked about user experience. You can bet that most of the smart business app makers have spent countless hours and capital making sure that the navigation or the journey, on their app is a welcoming and friendly one.

## Social Commitment

Many companies now are becoming socially conscious in the way that they go about their business. They're giving money back to society and to people in need. I think you're going to see more and more companies in the technology space, as well as other areas giving part of their hard-earned capital back to charity. As such, I think you should make that commitment with your own company. Embrace some specific charity that you know. Make that commitment very visible in all of your website communications, and so on.

> *6% of annual profits*
> *average amount SMBs give to charities*
> Source: US Small Business Association

This raises the bar. It keeps you competitive with many other businesses who are also doing the same. It would be a great way for you to enhance your brand as well as your ethical commitment to the community.

## Customer Relationship Management (CRM)

Another very important inflection point for any small business owner is that you must embrace and activate CRM. The key for any business to make the leap into a fully engaged technology commitment is to have CRM system. Our statistics tell us that about a third of small business owners are already there. If you're just kicking the tires on this, if there's one move you want to be sure to make in the next few months, it's to sign onto a CRM system.

It shouldn't be surprising that your customer database, your prospects, existing customers, and all of their contact information is a gigantic asset that you own. This is in addition to all the equipment, real estate and all the other obvious components of your asset base. But your customer list should be right there with all of those other assets. In order to leverage the value of these assets, you need a software system that will help you understand all the criteria and specific data points of your list.

You must have all of your contacts within a CRM system. That then becomes the anchor, the lifeblood, of everything else you do, whether it's social media marketing, online email newsletters, a blog or traditional mailing. The idea of using this as the central system for your business is absolutely essential in today's marketplace. The results it garners will allow you to gain insights on exactly how your prospects and customers are engaging your service. You can tell how many times customer A opened up your newsletter, visited your website, or used the coupons you sent.

All of these data points, these signals, will help you understand what's doing well in your business: what's selling, what's not selling, and how your customers prefer to hear from you. As much as the CRM system is needed to actually do all of this, the essential commitment you need to make is to actually analyze the data that comes out of the platform. That's the beauty of having an AppStack. This provides you with an understanding all the data coursing through your enterprise. It allows you to become more strategic and less reactive so you're not putting out fires on a daily basis.

Another important element of your digital sphere is to continue or start to do most of your procurement online. The days of having to fax or call in orders or wait for the sales rep on their weekly visit to your store are pretty much gone. Those old methods continue to increasingly become archaic - if you haven't already done so, let 'em go, already!

Embracing all purchasing online will save you time, and certainly allow products to be delivered to you just in time so you don't become a continual warehouse. There are so many smart systems now built into procurement software by your various vendors, you'll be amazed. You're going to save not only time, but space, as well as the shipping costs involved of returning product that has not been sold.

A perfect example is what Amazon is doing in regards to printing books. I don't have to go out and print 50,000 books ahead of our launch. The Amazon system actually allows us to print on demand. A customer like you may have bought this book in hardcover on Amazon. Behind the scenes, seamlessly, the book was printed when you made the order. This is a perfect example of real-time procurement, and it's happening across every vertical industry. Online procurement will be, if it isn't already, an essential part of your workday.

A real skill is the building of human connections within your network so that you've got the technical side very well-connected for real-time and expedited delivery, just like Amazon. You're able to have the Amazon experience—even better—where everything is well-connected. It will become so highly optimized that you'll find you've built your profit centers out with great strength.

One of our clients who owns several automotive repair shops said to us that he used to order too much product. The automotive aftermarket industry is one of the few markets that lars its product out shipping it back and forth. What this confirms is that many old-school procurement processes are taking guesses at how much product they need. This leads to them winding up having to ship the unused or unsold product back to the vendor.

All of these new procurement software systems—in varying degrees in various markets—have made an impact. They're really just reinventing the way one buys for one's business. Certainly the end game is savings—both time and money—and the saving of space within their office or building.

## Cybersecurity

You need to know as much as possible how secure your website, your data platforms, and your ecommerce systems are. Certainly, most of the vendors that you work with likely have done a great job in making sure that their systems are secure. It would benefit you greatly to go in and review their security and privacy policies. You can certainly call one of their customer service representatives and ask them to review the policies with you. Clearly, with the amount of cyberattacks going on—at least at large enterprise Fortune 500 companies—it's a very scary time.

While it's unlikely that small businesses will experience the same number of attacks, it's certainly happening and, thus, it's an imperative next step for you to understand how secure your systems are as you go about your business day.

Earlier, I reviewed best practices of some of the security systems and policies. Be sure to read all of the policies in your vendor's software.

## Analytics

This goes back to CRM. For every software solution you have in your stack, there's the ability to manage, assess, and monitor all of the data that's coursing through the system. As you begin to save time by using business apps to run your business, it's essential to have real-time access to these key metrics within each component software.

For instance, consider your website. Analyze the data around elements such as:

- Number of visitors
- What time they're coming into your site
- What parts of your site they're looking at

Within the executive dashboard of your site, you can see your data in real time. As you begin to build a ritual around looking at your data, you'll see trends emerging over time. Those insights will inform you as to what to change in your business.

Every one of your software partners can lead you to tutorials, as well as other educational platforms like webinars and white papers, so that you understand how to use that software better and how to mine that data even more effectively.

*Of small businesses who use small data:*
*83% use email marketing reports*
*64% use website analytics*
*52% use social media analytics*
*48 % use sales trends*

SOURCE: https://blogs.constantcontact.com/small-businesses-data/

Our company, SquareStack, was built with small business owners and their data in mind. We have automated a variety of processes and everyday business activities (ranging from a single sign to a multipurpose universal dashboard) but the highest value is the master dashboard. It aggregates all the critical real time data generated by your entire business. The insights extracted from your dashboard regularly inform you to improve the economies of scale within your company and ultimately, your businesses success.

As I mentioned earlier, I'm using 35+ business apps to run my business. I also know of companies that have 50 or 60 different pieces of software to build their business. At the end of the day, you have 20 different functions within a company, ranging from HR to real estate to project management. You really need one, or at most two to three per category, but there are some companies that use a few software solutions within certain functions.

When a company gets to 50-plus employees and multiple physical locations, they're ready to hire a deeper bench of IT talent and move into enterprise software solutions. My team and I built SquareStack for the 25 million small business owners who have 50 employees or less. SquareStack is not a solution for IBM or CVS. But for the many companies that make up the larger part of our economy, SquareStack absolutely can accommodate their needs.

## Metrics Dashboard

I provide a global view of all of the systems within your stack. This may include HR metrics, bank, credit card, a line of credit, and social media. It also offers Survey Monkey and expense management. Think about every segment of your enterprise that has a piece of software and metrics within it. The SquareStack solution brings all of that together in one visual of charts that show those key metrics. Imagine NASA control center: all those screens showing all the different data coming in from the systems within the rockets. Similarly, SquareStack shows all of the systems within your business enterprise.

*60%*
*SMBs that would prefer to work with a single provider*
SOURCE: LSA Tech Adoption Index Survey Wave II

It allows you to act in much the same way a global CEO of a Fortune 500 company does. You have a complete real-time handle on just what's going on in your business. Did that check come in at the bank? What's my line of credit balance? Did my reps submit their expense reports? Where's my product in the supply chain delivery system? How many people opened our newsletter? How many coupons are fulfilled on our ecommerce site? What would be better than an owner of a company knowing all that in real time? There's nothing better.

You're able to anticipate what your needs are and take advantage of this ever-changing world. The one thing that I realized over the years as a small business owner is that the only constant is change, as the ancient Greek philosopher Heraclitus stated. So how do you thrive in a constantly changing environment? You need to have something that will adapt and change with you.

It will be imperative for you to be able to address these metrics in your company, even as early as the startup stage.

## Simple Action Steps to Take Now

- Ask yourself what social mission you can adopt for your company. Pick a charity or good cause that you can be proud to align your company name with. Make a conscious decision to support that group and make it part of your DNA. Make sure you're not doing it for just the marketing advantages. Be authentic in the choice and commitment. If you can't do that, don't bother. From there, make sure you incentivize your team to support the cause, and weave into your communications that commitment.

- Review all your current business apps' analytics capabilities. Make sure they're all turned on and you have easy access to them. The vendors can certainly assist you in upgrading your understanding and provide insights on gathering ability for their solutions

- Check out our solution SquareStack as an option to manage all your business apps in one place and enjoy the power and easy access of a consolidated dashboard.

# MOVE FORWARD
## FEARLESSLY AND FOCUSED

Congratulations on making it to this last chapter. You have learned a great deal about the cloud and the emerging business app revolution. At the onset, you certainly had an inkling of just how rapidly this disruptive transformation is affecting the way I go about our work. By now, you may be taking a deep breath, and saying, "Wow! Can I commit to the necessary focus and energy needed to understand and utilize the required technology platforms of today's successful small to mid-sized business?"

The answer is yes. You made these first steps, and as many of our partners, friends, and peers in the small to mid-sized community, I empathize with the commitment needed. Thus, I'm not going to let you finish up these last few pages and then be on your way. Not a chance. I'd like to now share our own business in a bit more detail, and how it might help achieve success in this new age of the *AppStack*.

First, I encourage you to join our SquareStack "Roundtable", a community of small and mid-sized business owners. I call our software solution the Business Apps Command Center. It's a great platform on which you can house all of your business apps. It will help you save time every day, and see the real-time metrics needed to lead your business. I even have a social network within it. Here you can read business apps reviews and share your own stories, as well as check out analyses of apps you use.

We're an early-stage company, and in the spirit of the way businesses are launched in today's tech driven world, I want to come in at no charge for three months to test drive our solution. This approach will allow us to, provide insights and to bond with fellow small to mid-sized businesses. It's important, if not obvious, that I'm figuring out how technology and user-affinity evolves. There's no better way to do this than to crowdsource, and let the collective feedback serve as our master guiding light. While my team is darn smart, and our earliest champion users are darn sticklers, I know there's still a lot of work to do. Please join us!

I guarantee that you'll welcome our "Uber App" into your Stack. As our lives continue to become more and complex due to technology, I hope that the insights presented in this book will help you simplify your life. Balance in life is necessary. With the blurring of lines as to when to turn off and turn back on, it's too easy to get further muddled. If you can simplify technology rather than allow it to make your life more complex, you'll have succeeded.

When you register for SquareStack (www.squarestack.com), you'll receive our monthly newsletter on business apps tech tips, overall small business strategies and tactics, and shared technology success stories from our community. Also, I will have a regular schedule of webinars hosted by leading app makers in every category that matters to you and your business including finance, HR, marketing, CRM, Social, Website building and hosting.

Finally, you'll be able to submit your own questions and shared successes with our SquareStack RoundTable Advisors—made up in part of all those early beta users we wooed aboard in our early startup days.

Please go back to the AppStack Readiness Checklist at the beginning of this book and see where you scored. I guarantee if you devote an hour a week to learning more, and spend 15 to 30 minutes at the beginning of your day on your brand spanking new SquareStack Business Apps Command Center, you'll soon feel in control of your business in real time. Not only that, you'll feel a lot better that you're leaning forward into embracing and succeeding in this wild new era of the cloud. You'll become more durable, more balanced, and more successful.

*Appify* your business today, and you'll be the master of your destiny. You'll no longer be lost in regard to your many software tools. You'll leverage the power of all of your apps to gain extra time daily that you can use to innovate in your business, or just enjoy your personal time to pursue other passions.

You'll also find yourself constantly growing because you now have access to crucial real-time data from all areas of your business. Just like a Fortune 500 CEO, you'll be able monitor your business metrics. This will enable you to more quickly take advantage of your successes while avoiding potential failures. Take advantage of one of the best things that has ever happened for small businesses.

Here's to your success!

# APPENDIX

## SquareStack and our SquareStack Roundtable

My company, SquareStack, is what we call a "Business Apps Command Center" and I created it out of initial small business owners' insights. Nearly two years ago, I held a few days of focus groups. I recruited a dozen small business owners from a wide variety of industries and generations and asked them to share their technology challenges with us.

Our goal was to hear from peers about their technology challenges and how they go about their day using their digital devices, social media, and software. I had a hunch that they faced the same pains I experienced.

Our team spent more than 12 months working with our "SquareStack Circle" what many in my industry would call a beta user group. Before we launched the solution commercially, it was this group of owners who really led the way on what our solution should provide in terms of technology efficiency and user experience. They are still part of our team even today.

We started building a feature set that addressed those technology challenges. This led to what is called a wireframe, or a blueprint if you will, of what the tool would look like. We then brought it back to our user group and asked for more feedback. Next, we built what is called a minimum viable product (MVP). This included some workable tools and navigation, but it was still was a long way off from being market-ready. We still needed more user feedback.

We had a few more iterations—you get the picture—and one year later it was introduced it to the marketplace. I can vouch for many other app- makers who went down a similar path before they launched. One anecdote worth mentioning here is the story of Gmail. It was in beta for five years, and many of Google's current software launches will have the beta tag for quite some time.

While they're commercially open, users are paying real money for them. It's technically true that they can be in a perpetual beta stage as Google engineers are always adding, deleting, and tlaking features as data and customer feedback drive those improvements. On a somewhat ironic note, nostalgic Gmail users have an option to restore the beta logo on their user interface.

**Finally, I would like to extend a thank you for being one of our first readers by offering you a 90-day free trial of SquareStack once we launch to the consumer market this summer.  If you'd like to take advantage of this opportunity, just visit www.squarestack.com/90daysfree and provide us your name and email and enter code "AmazonAppify" and we will confirm your request.**

**Soon thereafter, you'll get a formal invite from us to register and get your own fully functional SquareStack account to build out your business dashboard and manage all your business apps from a Single Sign On username and password. Thank you again for your support and I hope you will take me up on my offer!**

# ACKNOWLEDGMENTS

To Melissa Wilson and her team at Networlding Publishing, for guiding this first-time author on this arduous but super fantastic journey from my chicken scratch journals to a well-honed, professionally guided content offering.

To my team at SquareStack and our investors who saw my vision for this emerging category and share the enthusiasm every day as we work together to help small business owners leverage technology to build their businesses and fulfill their dreams.

To our SquareStack Circle of Entrepreneurs—small business owners from diverse backgrounds and industries who spent a good amount of time helping us build our platform and provide me their first-hand insights into the workaday life of a small business owner.

To my Dad, Big Bill, who while not an entrepreneur, he was my biggest supporter and life mentor. Whenever one of my businesses was in a tailspin, he would always say: "Billy did you miss a meal?!" Never did, like he must have as a poor immigrant kid growing up in Chicago.

To Joe Pulizzi, accomplished author and entrepreneur, who encouraged me to write this book and whose own writings in Content Inc, informed me on how to deploy thought leadership content to build my business.

To Raman Chandra of Junto Institute, Jason Jacobson of Founder Institute and Steve Raquel, Adjunct Professor, College of Media Studies at my alma mater, University of

Illinois at Urbana-Champaign. All of you in your roles as mentors and leaders for entrepreneurs and digital media students have also guided me in this journey.

To my great family at Christ Church of Oak Brook. Our family has been blessed to be part of such a vibrant, intimate, and supportive community.

# RESOURCES AND REFERENCES

## Chapter 01

· Be sure to check out Salesforce's blog site as they share Small Business tech trends, interviews with owners and tech vendors. Great resource: https://www.salesforce.com/blog/

· G2 Crowd is the leading business software review company and has become a primary resource for those Small Business Owners researching new business apps. https://blog.g2crowd.com/blog/

· Capterra is another great business app review site. https://www.capterra.com/

· App Annie provides companies analytics and business app intelligence. https://www.appannie.com/en/

· Pew Center is our public repository that tracks just about every trend you can think of and make sure you check out their robust Internet and Technology section. http://www.pewinternet.org/

· Even if you're not a member, go to the National Federation of Independent-Business website and search for the latest peer driven research on technology adoption. https://www.nfib.com/business-resources

## Chapter 02

· App Annie is an app analytics and app market data firm that enables app activation and maintenance. https://www.appannie.com/en/

· While you likely aren't a developer, Intuit Developer website has a host of great research and trend data that will enlighten you. https://developer.intuit.com/app/developer/homepage

· Local Search Association (LSA.org) is a group of companies who sell to local businesses. Their Tech Adoption Trend reports, led by Charles Laughlin, are great insights into what small businesses are doing around technology. https://www.thelsa.org/lsa/tech-adoption-index.aspx

· Check out some of these incubators and accelerators. While these are Chicago based, most large cities have similar organizations.

-1871, Chicago's Technology & Entrepreneurship Center https://1871.com/
-Founder Institute, a business incubator, entrepreneur training, and startup launch program. In 180 cities around the world. https://fi.co/
-Junto Institute for Global Leadership  http://www.thejuntoinstitute.com/

· Amazon Web Services is the leader in the cloud; check out their LEARN center. https://aws.amazon.com/getting-started/?nc2=h_ql_gs

· SmallBiztrends is a well-regarded media company serving the small business community, plenty of strategic and how to advice, not just on technology, but with everyday challenges. https://smallbiztrends.com/

# Chapter 03

· Visit our company website to learn more about how to build your AppStack. http://squarestack.com/

· For a resource more focused on marketing technology, go to https://chiefmartec.com/

· For what small business marketers are focusing on when it comes to our overall market segment, B2SMB Institute is worth a visit. https://b2smbi.com/

· For good hands on information on the integrated small business enterprise, go to https://fitsmallbusiness.com/

· Visit the FCC and SBA websites for great tips on cybersecurity:
https://www.fcc.gov/general/cybersecurity-small-business
https://www.sba.gov/managing-business/cybersecurity/
top-ten-cybersecurity-tips

· Here are a handful of comprehensive resources about data privacy best practices:
https://www.privacytrust.com/guidance/
https://thedma.org/resources/privacy-resources/

# Chapter 04

· For more information on user experience go to: https://uxplanet.org/

· B2B Marketing, a global media company for business marketers has a comprehensive library of guides and research on Customer and User Experience. https://www.b2bmarketing.net/en/free-downloadable-guides/customer-experience
· The User Experience design Professional Association. Chock full of resources:
https://uxpa.org/

· To learn about analytics and how to leverage their insights, check out these informative sites:
https://www.digitalanalyticsassociation.org/
https://www.tableau.com/community
https://www.fundera.com/blog/web-analytics-tools

· Inc.com has a series of newsletters and a section devoted to big data for small business:
https://www.inc.com/data-detectives

# Chapter 05

· Check out the National Federation of Independent Business (NFIB) website and specifically their research and trends page. It's worth joining the organization too: https://www.nfib.com/foundations/research-center/

· Reid Hoffman, CEO and founder of LinkedIn, wrote a fantastic book, *The Startup of You*, on "the solopreneur," and what it means to manage your career as if it were a small business: http://www.thestartupofyou.com/

· It's revealing to see how companies market to small business. Check out these resources:
https://www.b2bmarketing.net/en-gb/search/site/SME
https://www.americanexpress.com/en-us/business/trends-and-insights/

· Need to know more about the gig economy? Here are a few references:
https://hbr.org/2018/03/thriving-in-the-gig-economy
https://www.amazon.com/Gig-Economy-Complete-Getting-Financing-ebook/dp/B01HJ35YPG

· When it comes to user experience, be sure to check out usability.gov:
https://www.usability.gov/what-and-why/user-experience.html

# Chapter 06

· For a complete overview of all things SaaS, Amazon Marketplace is a great resource: https://aws.amazon.com/marketplace

· A comprehensive library on SaaS at Apprenda: https://apprenda.com/library/software-on-demand/

· For accounting alone, QuickBooks has a diverse library of SaaS based business apps: https://apps.intuit.com/app/apps/home

· G2 Crowd has a layman's guide to SaaS: https://learn.
g2crowd.com/what-is-saas
· Build your own app? Yes, there is now an App Institute:
https://appinstitute.com/

## Chapter 07

· Expand your knowledge on the difference between
strategy and tactics. Subscribe to a Harvard Business
Review newsletter: https://hbr.org/topic/strategic-planning

· Forbes.com has a dedicated section for entrepreneurs
and strategy is a frequent topic: https://www.forbes.com/
entrepreneurs/#2ed340753035

· Here are a few books on strategy that every entrepreneur
should read:
> *The Art of War* by Sun Tzu
> *The Prince* by Niccolò Machiavelli
> *The Strategy Paradox* by Michael Raynor
> *Blue Ocean Strategy* by W. Chan Kim & Renèe
> Mauborgne
> *Good to Great* by Jim Collins

· Google "to do software" and try one of these business
apps to build a more efficient work day

## Chapter 08

Expand your understanding of each of the high C's:

· Collect data: https://www.sba.gov/advocacy/small-
business-data-resources

· Capitalize Finance online: https://www.business.com/ articles/5-fintech-trends-smbs-need-to-embrace/
· Competition: https://smallbiztrends.com/2009/11/ competitive-intelligence-tools-for-smbs.html

· Curricula: https://business.udemy.com/

· Content and Curation: https://contentmarketinginstitute. com/
· Cost Per: Demand Generation and how to perfect it: https://www.demandgenreport.com/

· Cloud Ubiquity: https://www.thelsa.org/lsa/tech-adoption-index.aspx

· Commerce: Communities to learn more about ecommerce: https://ecommerce-platforms.com/ecommerce-selling-advice/ecommerce-forums-communities

· Community: https://www.higherlogic.com/home

· Customer Relationship Management: A beginner's guide: https://zapier.com/learn/crm/what-is-a-crm/

· Collaboration: PC Magazine's 2018 Report: https://www. pcmag.com/article2/0,2817,2489110,00.asp

· Conscious: Learn more about being a socially conscious company: https://www.entrepreneur.com/article/294421

· Cynic: Choosing the right apps: https://www.inc.com/

cox-business/how-to-choose-the-right-technology-for-your-small-business-or-startup.html

· Cyber: Security always needs attention, from the SBA: https://www.sba.gov/managing-business/cybersecurity/top-ten-cybersecurity-tips

## Chapter 09

· Want your website built in an hour? Check out GoDaddy: https://www.godaddy.com/websites/website-builder

· Newsletters are a core marketing tool for small businesses. Check out these resources:
https://www.constantcontact.com/
https://smallbiztrends.com/2018/06/email-newsletter-best-practices-small-business.html
https://blog.hubspot.com/marketing/email-marketing-guide

· Looking for a digital geek? Finding one is as simple as a search on a job site! https://www.indeed.com/q-Digital-Geek-jobs.html

· Listen to Barry Moltz on the radio for lots of advice around technology and running a small business: https://barrymoltz.com/small-business-radio-show/

· Check out your local business journal for seminars, or your local chamber of commerce:
https://acbj.com/ and https://www.uschamber.com/

· Here are the best in business apps reviews:
https://www.g2crowd.com/

https://www.capterra.com/
https://www.getapp.com/
http://squarestack.com/

## Chapter 10

·  Aligning with a charity:
https://www.charitynavigator.org/
https://www.businessnewsdaily.com/1604-choosing-
business-charity.html

·  Understanding analytics:
https://hbr.org/2015/10/5-essential-principles-for-
understanding-analytics
https://www.youtube.com/watch?v=GRp8oH7f1rY

## Chapter 11

·  Go to SquareStack registration: https://app.squarestack.
com/register?get_started=true

# FOOTNOTES

[1] Intuit Developer Blog April 15, 2017

[2] Psychology Today September 19, 2009

[3] Data from App Annie, February 2018

[4] http://cyber-gear.com/main/mobile-apps.php

[5] https://blog.rackspace.com/

[6] www.businessnewsdaily.com May 10, 2018

[7] www.smallbiztrends.com October 2018

# ABOUT THE AUTHOR

Bill Furlong is a serial entrepreneur and currently serves as an advisor, mentor and investor in a variety of data and B2B centric early and mid-stage companies. He is the founder and CEO of SquareStack. Billed as SMB's Business Apps Command Center, the firm helps small business owners navigate the technology gauntlet, consolidating their diverse cloud-based software applications and providing software reviews for greater ROI and success in their own ventures.

Before that, he was part of founding team of Bizo, an audience data management platform firm, which was acquired by LinkedIn. Serving as SVP/Business Development, he and his team built Bizo's data network of over 2,500 business media websites, and brokered new data agreements with Fortune 500 companies such as GE, Oracle, Dow Jones, and Time-Warner.

Bill was also founder and CEO of B2BWorks, the first B2B online ad network at the onset of Web 1.0. Prior to that, he was managing director of *BtoB Magazine* and its website, and held various management roles for the Advertising Age Group/Crain Communications, for over a decade.

A graduate of the College of Media Studies of the University of Illinois at Urbana–Champaign, Bill remains active in UIUC alumni association activities and serves as a visiting lecturer at its College of Media. He is a member of the Chicago 16" Softball Hall of Fame, and an alum of the Second City Improvisational School. Bill lives in Clarendon Hills, Illinois, with his wife, Peggy; their children Liam, Kylie, and Conor; and their dog, Piper.

www.ingramcontent.com/pod-product-compliance
Lightning Source LLC
Chambersburg PA
CBHW071550200326
41519CB00021BB/6681